W9-CJY-662

The Uncorrupted Heart

The Uncorrupted Heart JOURNAL AND LETTERS OF FREDERICK JULIUS GUSTORF 1800-1845

EDITED, WITH INTRODUCTION
AND NOTES BY FRED GUSTORF
TRANSLATED FROM THE
GERMAN BY FRED GUSTORF
AND GISELA GUSTORF

UNIVERSITY OF MISSOURI PRESS
COLUMBIA, MISSOURI
1969

Standard Book Number 8262–8812–X
Library of Congress Card Number 70–93049
Printed in the United States of America
Copyright © 1969 by
The Curators of the University of Missouri

That they may know and appreciate their pioneer
heritage this book is affectionately dedicated
to the descendants of Frederick Julius Gustorf
and Harriet Benson his "charming Englishwoman"

Preface

It is impossible to remember when, as a child, I first became aware of a brownish bundle of paper, folded lengthwise and tied with an old brown ribbon, which was kept in the bottom drawer of an English walnut chest in one of the bedrooms of our home and reverently described by my elders as "The Diary." No member of the family had read it because neither the writer's widow nor his three children were able to read the concise German script in which it was written.

Other circumstances contributed to the family's seeming neglect of these papers. During World War I, for example, it was considered bad taste to express more than a casual interest in one's German ancestry, and during the early Nazi era and World War II, the need to explain the source of a German name was sometimes embarrassing, especially when one's military duties were of a highly sensitive nature.

Although the diary and other personal papers of Frederick Julius Gustorf, my German-born great-grandfather, passed into my hands upon the death of his granddaughter, Alice M. Gustorf, in 1951, I was too preoccupied at the time with personal problems to give much thought to family history, German or otherwise. When the Army ordered me to Germany in 1955, I could easily, before going abroad, have determined my forefather's place of birth and obtained enough background information from his personal papers to provide a starting point for research, should I want to look into my family's history. But although the war had ended ten years earlier, I felt extremely reluctant to engage in any activity that might place my sensitive assignment in jeopardy. True, my inquiries could have been pursued in a discreet manner that would not have aroused suspicion or led to a charge of fraternization, but without Frederick Gustorf's identification papers there was no simple way of determining his place of birth. I might, to be sure, have examined closely a map of West Germany, in the hope that the name of some obscure town might provide a clue, but I thought in all probability the birthplace was now within the boundaries of East Germany, and therefore inaccessible. Imagine my chagrin when I discovered, after returning to the United States and examining his passport, that my great-grandfather was born in Cassel, then capital of the Kingdom of Westphalia and now known as Kassel, the seat of government of the West German state of Hesse. The city is a mere 115 miles north of my military station at Frankfurt/Main by autobahn, and I had spent the night there several times in the course of my official Army duties.

But an even greater surprise was in store for me. Further examination of his passport revealed that he had lived for ten years in Frankfurt/Main, within the confines of the Old City. This knowledge would have had little more than sentimental value in any search undertaken during my Frankfurt tour for, without the specific information that I obtained later from the Frankfurt archives, I could have done little more than explore the areas that would have been familiar to him.

In 1961, three years after my retirement from the Army, I made a special trip to Frankfurt for the purpose of examining records of my ancestor that my German friend Dr. Joachim Fischer had found in the city's archives. Included in these papers were the annual applications from Frederick Julius Gustorf to the Frankfurt Senate for permission to teach the English language to residents of the city. From these applications I was able to obtain five different addresses where he had lived during his residence of ten years, one of which my son and I had passed at least a dozen times en route to and returning from points south of the Main River.

Despite its faded ink and difficult Sütterlin script, the 120-year-old diary has yielded the secrets of its writer through the determined efforts of its translator, the diarist's great-granddaughter-in-law.

F.G.

San Francisco, California
May, 1969

Contents

The Uncorrupted Heart

Introduction

Frederick Julius Gustorf sailed from Le Havre on August 1, 1834, on the American packet *Yazoo*. He was thirty-four years of age and, according to his passport, issued by the Free City of Frankfurt am Main on June 24, 1833, he was described as being five "shoe" six inches in height, with brown hair, eyebrows and beard, an open forehead, blue eyes, medium nose and mouth, round chin and oval face, and a healthy complexion. He used eyeglasses. As an officially approved teacher of the English language residing temporarily in Frankfurt, Herr Gustorf was originally granted permission to travel to Baden-Baden, for use of the baths, and farther on, to Strasbourg. The passport requested, on the bearer's behalf, freedom of movement and the protection of civil and military authorities. Indorsements of the document, dated in July, verify his progress up the Rhine from Mainz, through Germersheim to Strasbourg, thence to Baden-Baden and Carlsruhe.[1]

A year later, June 3, 1834, Gustorf had his passport extended for six additional months and validated for travel to Paris; he obtained French and Bavarian visas at the same time. His route from Frankfurt was via Heilbronn, Stuttgart, and Strasbourg, but, since he did not reach Paris until July 24, it is probable that, en route, Gustorf toured the Upper Rhine and Lake Constance region, then known as Rheinbayern. His leisurely approach to the port suggests that a round of farewell visits to relatives and friends was a partial motive for his travels. Probably his mother was then living in Strasbourg. Significantly, no visit to his native city Hessen-Cassel is in the record of this journey and probably none was made, although his younger brothers Lazarus and Maurice were businessmen there. His sister Adelaide had married a successful lawyer and was living in Rotenburg on the Fulda, southeast of Cassel. Another sister, Marianna, an invalid whose principal source of support was Lazarus,

---

[1] Prior to 1900, many German cities like Kassel, Karlsruhe, Köln, and Koblenz were spelled with a C.

3

probably lived with her brother in Cassel. Ludwig, the eldest brother, had become estranged from the family and was living permanently in Berlin where, in 1883, he was appointed Royal Prussian Privy Councilor of Medicine, elevated to the Prussian nobility, and authorized a family coat of arms.

A letter dated March 5, 1884, to Harriet Benson Gustorf from her husband's nephew Julius Gustorf, a resident of Cöln, bore news of the family in Germany, including word of the honor bestowed upon the eldest and only surviving German brother-in-law; the youngest and only other living member of the once large family, Adelaide, was still residing in Rotenburg. Verification of the status of Ludwig Christian Nikolaus von Gustorf appears in *Gothaisches Genealogisches Taschenbuch der Briefadeligen Häuser*, first (1907), 245, and fifth (1911), 342, editions: "Evangelical.—The family stems from the Lower Rhine.—Prussian nobility Berlin 13 February 1883 (to Dr. Ludwig Christian Nikolaus Gustorf, Royal Prussian Privy Councilor of Medicine in Berlin).—Coat of arms (1883): Twice divided (horizontally); above on a black background a narrow red vertical bar over a wide silver panel; center on a blue background, a left-facing silver hound with gold collar; below a green clover leaf against a gold background. Above the golden-crowned, silver helmet with blue visors, a left-facing silver hound's head with gold collar."

Had he been living in 1883, Frederick Julius would have experienced little satisfaction from this knowledge that his brother in Berlin had been honored by Kaiser Wilhelm I, but his descendants are grateful for the distinction, since it included information concerning the family's origins, which otherwise would not have been recorded. The same genealogical source names Max Joseph Gustorf as Stammvater or ancestor of record. He is described as Catholic by faith and banker by profession. The place and date of his birth are not parts of the record, but Cassel is listed as his place of death, date unknown. His wife's maiden name was Leopoldine von Arnstein. Max Joseph and Leopoldine Gustorf of Cassel are presumed, therefore, to have been the grandparents of Frederick Julius Gustorf, and Max Joseph is further presumed to have been the family stem from the Lower Rhine, specifically the town of Gustorf, about forty kilometers west of Düsseldorf, from which two of three distantly related families of that name are known to have migrated upriver in the eighteenth century, one to Cöln and the other to

4

Cassel. Source of this information was Dr. Wilhelm Gustorf (no relation), Chief Justice of the County Court in Düsseldorf.

The father of Frederick Julius Gustorf had failed in the banking business in 1816, following the defeat of Napoleon I at Leipzig and the dissolution of the French-oriented Kingdom of Westphalia, which had been ruled from Cassel from 1807 to 1813 by Napoleon's brother Jerome Bonaparte, a puppet king. It was his father's wish that, upon completion of his education at age sixteen, Frederick Julius should become apprentice to a linen draper or cloth manufacturer and ultimately contribute to the family income. But the second son had been educated with his brothers and sisters by a private tutor, and the prospect of entering a trade was repugnant to him, all his tastes being literary. Understandably, family relations became somewhat strained, and in 1819 the youth, accompanied by a friend from Cassel, made his first voyage to the United States of America. The exact date of his arrival is unknown. However, the Harvard College catalog for the academic year 1820–21 lists Frederick J. Gustorf as "Private Teacher in German," which meant that he was authorized to teach the German language to Harvard students privately, making all arrangements, including fees, with each student individually. The listing does not appear in subsequent catalogs, however, because another German was appointed to the Harvard faculty for the purpose of conducting classes in the German language, a post Frederick Julius undoubtedly had hoped to obtain; nevertheless, he continued tutoring privately at Harvard and also at Yale for the next four years, although he was never mentioned in the catalog of the New Haven institution.

It is reasonable to assume that, while living in Boston and New Haven, the young man visited other cities on the Atlantic Coast, including Philadelphia, where his friend and shipmate from Cassel, G. D. Rosengarten, had established a chemical laboratory.[2] On November 14, 1822, in fact, he declared on oath before the Clerk of the Mayor's Court for the City of Philadelphia "that it was bona fide his intention to become a citizen of the United States and to renounce forever all allegiance and fidelity to any foreign prince, potentate, state, or sovereignty whatsoever, and particularly to the Elector of Hesse of whom he was a Subject."

[2] Desilver's *Philadelphia Directory and Stranger's Guide*, 1833.

Regardless of his intentions with respect to United States citizenship, after a residence of five years the young Hessian returned suddenly to his native city, apparently intending to remain only a brief period. Perhaps he was suddenly homesick for Germany. It is more likely, however, that Frederick Julius had been summoned to a family conference in Cassel precipitated by some crisis—perhaps the serious illness or death of the father. The traveler carried a certificate signed by Samuel J. Prescott, Notary Public, Justice of the Peace, and Quorum, at Boston on June 18, 1824, which states that Mr. Frederick J. Gustorf, age twenty-four, height five feet eight and one-half inches, complexion light, eyes dark, "is a citizen of Hessen Cassel in Germany, and a gentleman of respectability to me well known. He has resided in the United States for about five years last past, and is now about to return to Germany; and all States, Potentates, and others whom it may concern, are requested to permit him to pass safely and freely, without giving, or permitting to be given to him any hindrance, but, on the contrary, affording to him all aid and protection, as would be done in like case for all those who may be recommended to the United States." The document bears indorsements indicating that the bearer reached Rotterdam on August 10 and Cassel on August 16, 1824.

If the family crisis that brought Frederick Julius home so hurriedly was in fact concerned with the serious illness or death of the head of the family, one must assume that the youth promised his mother, brothers, and sisters that he would abandon, or at least postpone, his plans for becoming an American citizen. Circumstances strongly suggest that the terms of the father's will imposed certain conditions upon this "prodigal son," to be fulfilled by him to the complete satisfaction of the other surviving members of the family in order to qualify for his share of the estate. This premise is supported by later events of record, which indicate that the conditions required this son to remain in his homeland for at least the next ten years.

Whatever conditions may have been imposed, they evidently did not require his residence and employment in Cassel, because in January, 1825, Frederick Julius applied to the Senate of the Free City of Frankfurt for permission to reside there and teach the English language; his petition was sponsored by the Frankfurt Envoy from the Court of the Elector of Hessen-Cassel. In support of his application, Herr Gustorf submitted letters of recommenda-

6

tion from the presidents of both Harvard and Yale, together with a letter from the editor of *The North American Review,* a promising new literary magazine published in Boston. The application is preserved in the Frankfurt archives, together with Herr Gustorf's annual requests for permission to remain in the city. The last application for renewal of his permit is dated August 1, 1833. The file also contains a certificate from the School and Church Commission of Frankfurt indicating that, at the request of the Senate, the applicant was examined on his knowledge of the English language.

During his ten-year residence in Frankfurt am Main, Frederick Julius Gustorf changed his living quarters five times, as revealed by his annual requests for permission to remain in the city. All were within the area now known as the Old City and in walking distance of the historic Römerhill and the Kaisersaal. Four of the five were private homes or privately operated rooming houses, and the fifth was a Gasthaus or tavern. His longest stay (four years) was at 71 Schnurgasse, only a block from Paulskirche and around the corner from the Kaisersaal. During his last two years in Frankfurt he lived at 11 Langestrasse, opposite the Heilige Geist hospital and two blocks from the Main River. Only two of these five addresses can be identified today in the reconstructed city, the Old City having been bombed into oblivion during the final years of World War II and replaced by modern multiple dwellings, apartments, and office buildings. Schnurgasse has been widened considerably and renamed Berliner Strasse; the postwar pile of rubble that was formerly 11 Langestrasse has been removed and now a modern nurses' dormitory stands in its place. In 1961, while this building was under construction, a part of the original brick-and-stone structure that had survived the holocaust was occupied by a furniture repair shop on the ground floor. A room on the second floor, facing the street, certainly was similar to, if not identical with, that in which my ancestor lived, impatiently awaiting the end of a ten-year exile and his return to the United States, where important unfinished business was pending in the Mayor's Court of Philadelphia.

The departure from Le Havre must have been a nostalgic experience, for the traveler knew it was unlikely he would ever see his relatives and friends in Germany again. Aboard ship he paid 650 francs for passage "in the cabin of the *Yazoo* from Havre to New York, including stores and all the comforts, the same as on the regular Packets between Havre & New York." The receipt for payment bears the signature of Henry Parker, captain of the vessel, and the place and date, Havre, August 1, 1834. Herr Gustorf was carrying a draft, purchased from M. A. v. Rothschild in Frankfurt on May 14, 1834, in the amount of 12,000 gulden (about $5,000), payable on sight in foreign currency at par. From New York he proceeded, not to his former haunts in Cambridge, Boston, and New Haven, but to the Rosengarten home at 24 Palmyra Row in Philadelphia.

On the advice of this friend, Frederick Julius cashed his sight draft and deposited the proceeds in three Philadelphia banks. The interest therefrom, about $300 annually, was his only source of income, and of that investment he lost every penny in the depression that followed the financial panic of 1837. Although he had lived modestly in Frankfurt, it would have been impossible to accumulate $5,000 in ten years by teaching English to German students. Undoubtedly this $5,000, or a major part thereof, was a conditional legacy from his deceased father that delayed his return to the United States for at least ten years.

His next move was significant in that it represented a clean break with the past and bespoke his plans for the future. Less than two months after departing Havre, he petitioned the Mayor's Court of Philadelphia for United States citizenship and was naturalized on September 27, 1834.

The history of the first thirty-four years of this young German's life is necessarily brief because it is reconstructed almost entirely from existing public and private records, which provide very little insight into motives and aspirations. For example: Why did he terminate his intellectual association with Harvard and Yale colleges to hurry back to Cassel in the summer of 1824? If it was "bona fide his intention" in 1822 to become a citizen of the United States, what influences prevailed upon him to remain in Germany for ten years before returning to America? Why, after obtaining his citizenship in Philadelphia, did he not resume his professional and scholastic associations in the cultural and literary environs of Cambridge and New Haven?

The suggestion has been made previously that the hurried trip from Boston to Cassel in 1824 was an involuntary action brought about by compassionate circumstances and that the ten-year sojourn in Frankfurt was in the nature of a probationary or "cooling-off" period imposed by authority of a family council. Voluntary or involuntary, Julius' absence from the intellectual communities of New England for a decade would have made it very difficult if not impossible for him to resume the status he had enjoyed as the first unofficial German language teacher at Harvard College. Furthermore, he was undoubtedly aware that one Karl Follen had joined the faculty in 1825 as the first regularly appointed instructor in the German language.[3] As a matter of fact, it is possible that Follen's appointment may have had some bearing upon Gustorf's sudden departure for Germany. He may have hoped to obtain the position that he saw was going to another, or he may have realized that, with Follen's appointment, tutoring services would no longer be needed.

On the other hand, considering his penchant for change and adventure, his teaching seems to have been a means for support while he waited to put into operation some long-anticipated but unavoidably postponed plan. A letter to his future wife, written at Philadelphia on February 4, 1837, a few months before their marriage, expresses the controlled impatience he endured while waiting out the ten probationary years in Frankfurt as well as during the frustrating weeks that delayed their reunion:

> "But very fine indeed to preach patience to others when we have got none ourselves, & I am one of those, so that when I am anxiously waiting for something, I wish to possess it already, when I am scheming something, that something shall be accomplished already, when something is drawing near, be it storm or sunshine, I long to be immerged in it already, without any care or puzzling of the brain, for these last, I never could bear, which is partly originating from the circumstances that during the more active part of my life, and when moving in the sphere allotted to me, every thing went smooth enough & I never knew what real crosses were."

And one of the things he had "schemed" and so anxiously desired to accomplish was, beyond doubt, an inspection of the German immigrant colonies in Illinois and Missouri, especially those areas described by the German writer Gottfried Duden, in his *Report*

[3] *German Culture in America, 1600–1900* (Madison, 1957), by Dr. Henry A. Pochmann, University of Wisconsin.

upon a Journey to the Western States of America, published privately in Elberfeld in 1829 and eagerly read by thousands of Germans who, like the writer, were unhappy with the political situation in Germany.

The most convenient and economical means of travel from Philadelphia to St. Louis were the canal and river boats via Pittsburgh, Cincinnati, and Louisville, but this route could not be used until late spring. Gustorf's journey began on May 9, 1835, with an all-day ride on the newly completed Columbia Railroad from Philadelphia to Columbia on the Susquehanna River eighty miles to the west. He intended to record his progress and observations in what he called his "traveling journal," designed to interest his friends and members of his own family, when he had one; it might even be published in some newspaper or magazine in Germany. The impressions of other German travelers in America, including Duden, Dr. Henry C. Gerke, and the distinguished young scholar Francis Lieber, had been widely read in Europe. In Philadelphia he had met the English political writer Harriet Martineau, who was gathering material for her *Society in America* (1837) and her *Retrospect of Western Travel* (1838), both published in London.

Personal accounts of the experiences and impressions of travelers have, for many generations, provided rich and varied records of peoples and places. The following materials present a view of the American Midwest in the first half of the nineteenth century as seen through the warmly expectant, then coolly objective, eyes of a young European.

Trip from **Philadelphia** to the **Western States,** and Stay in the **German Colonies** in **Illinois** and **Missouri**

The Traveling Journal

May 9, 1835. Left Philadelphia at nine o'clock in the morning by the Columbia Rail Road; arrived at five o'clock in the afternoon in Columbia on the Susquehanna River, whence we continued our trip by canal boat to Pittsburgh. Everywhere the country is well cultivated. Several towns, Coatesville in particular, are very prettily located; the banks of the Susquehanna are charming. On both sides of the river are high mountains with thick black forests. Occasionally there are small settlements or clearings. Near Marietta, a high and majestic group of rocks. The canal runs alongside the river. Facilities on board the boat, considering its narrow beam, are pretty good and, if there are not too many travelers, it is comfortable. The table is well laid out and loaded with choice food. En route I made the acquaintance of the sculptor, Persico, whom I saw last winter in Washington.[1] During our conversation he said that he intends to return to Europe in the near future. He complained of the lack of comfort in this country, and when the subject of our conversation shifted to women, he said in the typical Italian manner: "Les femmes aiment avec la tête et non avec le coeur"—a very true statement when you know the coldness

---

[1] According to Oliver W. Larkin, in *Art and Life in America,* Luigi Persico was one of the foreign artisans employed by Thomas Jefferson to carve Washington's stone statues and ornaments. Persico designed an eastern pediment for the Capitol. His design was modified in deference to the artistic tastes of President John Quincy Adams.

of American women. Again I must mention the banks of the river, charming wild land formerly inhabited by wild Indians. On the banks of this river lived "Gertrude of Wyoming" who was immortalized by the English poet, Campbell.[2]

May 10.   I was interrupted in my contemplation last night by the commotion of making up the beds in the cabin. On each side they made up fifteen in three rows, one on top of the other, and so we slept one above the other, hammock fashion. I had a very uncomfortable night because of insufficient space and fresh air. About two o'clock in the morning, one of the passengers discovered that his suitcase containing money was missing. Everybody left the cabin to check on his own possessions. When I returned to the room, my space was taken by somebody else and I had to spend the rest of the night on a table. Before dawn I went on deck. The canal is still running parallel to the Susquehanna. The riverbanks are still heavily wooded, as are the mountains. It is wild, romantic, and charming, but very rough and cold. What climate! As cold in spring as in December and quite different from spring in European areas. Everything is green, but only a few flowers can be seen and only a few birds' voices can be heard. Toward six o'clock in the morning we crossed the Susquehanna on a long covered bridge where, on the left bank, the canal parallels another river, the Juniata. The banks of this river also are hilly and covered with forests; here and there the forest is cleared and the land is pretty well cultivated.

---

[2] Thomas Campbell (1777–1844), one of England's minor poets, was considered a master of battle verse. His "Gertrude of Wyoming" commemorated the desolation of the immigrant colony at Wyoming, Pennsylvania, on the banks of the Susquehanna River, by Indians in 1778. The colony was known as "one of the happiest spots of human existence, for the hospitable and innocent manners of the inhabitants, the beauty of the country, and the luxuriant fertility of the soil and climate." Although this poem was described by a critic as the "clumsiest caricature of Spenserian stanza ever achieved by a man of real poetic power," its popular appeal, especially to European immi-

From the deck I can hear the morning church service below.
Some preacher or missionary happens to be among the passengers, and at once they had to use his professional services.
In this area fifty years ago the Delawares and the Miamis were
in undisputed possession of the land, but now there is no
sign of them. In the afternoon we skirted the Tuscarora
mountains, a chain of high, heavily forested areas with marvelous views—the most beautiful I have seen in America so
far. The small village of Mifflintown is located most pic-
turesquely on the slope above a bridge over the Juniata.

May 11.   Still the same scenery: forest after forest,
magnificent mountain ravines and fertile valleys. Between six
and seven o'clock, over the Juniata on a covered bridge again,
the canal continues. Cold, very cold, but cheerful and beautiful
sunshine. The inland transportation facilities of this country
are indeed very beautiful. It is very striking that in such fertile
areas as these there are so many hovels. Toward noon the
weather is warm and friendly—a spring day. Between Petersburg and Alexandria the mountains withdraw to the background, the valley widens more and more, the land is fertile,
and nice houses can be seen now and then. Here the words of
Byron come to me spontaneously: "The heartiest breast its
wish might bound, through life to dwell delighted here." As
he travels on, one is surprised at the great structure of the
canal. One moment you are on the Juniata itself and then you
are on the canal again, which flows across a bridge above the

---

grants, is understandable. For illustration, Part I, Stanza iv, appears below:
    And scarce had Wyoming of war or crime
    Heard, but in transatlantic story rung,
    For here the exile met from every clime,
    And spoke in friendship every distant tongue:
    Men from the blood of warring Europe sprung
    Were but divided by the running brook;
    And happy where no Rhenish trumpet sung,
    On plains no sieging mine's volcano shook,
    The blue-eyed German changed his sword to pruning-hook.

river. Three horses are always hitched to the boat and they are
changed every eight to ten miles.

May 12. About nine o'clock last night we arrived in
Hollidaysburg, where we remained aboard the canal boat until
dawn; then we continued by railroad. The night was very
unpleasant on account of the crowded cabin, which can't be
helped with so many passengers. Most of my traveling companions are storekeepers, lawyers, and a few ministers. The
lawyers and ministers are en route to the Far West, but they
do not have a definite destination. The whole day through
thick forests, devastated here and there by fire and axe. At the
bend of the little Conemaugh River, which winds its way
through the woods on my left, a wild and daring region appears.
The river disappears from my view as we pass over a steep, high
precipice through an opening in the wall of rock. Unexpectedly
we see the river again after it made a bend of one and a half
miles through a deep, narrow gorge, almost making a complete
circle, which can be seen from a high bridge over which the
railroad runs. It is a pity that here, as everywhere, much of the
beauty of the area is spoiled by cutting and burning of the
trees, which are scattered everywhere, too heavy to be moved.
This afternoon we have traveled not only above, but under
the Allegheny Mountains. We went through a tunnel 900
feet long and arrived in Johnstown toward sundown, one
hundred miles from Pittsburgh.[3] From there we traveled
aboard the canal boat *Cincinnati.* Johnstown is located very

---

[3] The combination of canal boat and rail transportation between Philadelphia
and Pittsburgh is described in Robert Selph Henry, *Trains* (Bobbs-Merrill,
Indianapolis, 1934), 12: "As late as 1834, the Philadelphia & Columbia Railroad, which was opened in that year, advertised that 'The locomotive engine
built by M. W. Baldwin, of this City, will depart daily when the weather is
fair, with a train of passenger's cars. On rainy days, horses will be attached.'
"This Philadelphia & Columbia Railroad was the first link in the 'Main
Line of Public Works' of the State of Pennsylvania, designed to connect Philadelphia with the waters of the Ohio River at Pittsburgh, in competition with
New York's Erie Canal. This remarkable scheme of transportation started with
a railroad across the ridge of land between the Schuylkill River at Philadelphia

beautifully in a valley and on a basin of water which forms a part of the canal.

May 13. Before sunrise. It is cold and very foggy. The fog is coming from the steadily widening Conemaugh, which flows toward the Mississippi Valley. Here we are going through another tunnel. The river bends for about one and a half miles, from which point we turn to the right and continue along the canal, which here runs between a high mountain and a rock: a so-called tunnel 800 feet in length. At the end of this tunnel, suddenly and unexpectedly, we see again the river that we just left. We crossed this river once over a beautifully built bridge and continued along the canal. At eight in the morning we reached the Kiskemitas, along the banks of which one sees many salt mines. This stream empties into the Allegheny. A marvelous view. Here the canal crosses the Allegheny over a handsome bridge in a setting of heavy woods and winding valleys, truly a majestic scene. A few hundred steps farther lies Freeport, a blooming little town that has been in existence only since the canal was built. The banks of the Allegheny are high and heavily wooded. Many coal mines are in operation here. Eight or ten miles from the town of Pittsburgh the area becomes more and more picturesque and the river gets wider and wider. One sees islands here and there. Now the riverbanks and the canal are lined with impressive estates and respectable houses. Now there was a heavy rain that, with the mist rising from the river, obscured the view. At eight o'clock in the

---

and the Susquehanna River. From there the passengers went on by canal-boat to the foot of the main ridge of the Alleghany [*sic*] Mountains. The next fifty-seven miles was the Portage Railroad, which climbed the mountain with a series of 'inclined planes' on which the cars were pulled up by stationary engines and cables, and let down by gravity. Besides cars there were wheeled 'cradles' upon which 'jointed' sections of the canal boats were dragged over the mountain without having to unload and reload the freight they carried— a remarkable arrangement much marvelled at at the time. On this railroad, four miles east of Johnstown, Pennsylvania, was a tunnel nine hundred and one feet long, the first railroad tunnel built in America. From the western foot of the mountains the traveler went on by canal boat to Pittsburgh."

evening the town of Pittsburgh was visible. Now the boat again crosses the Allegheny over a bridge one half mile in length. At the end of this bridge we saw something very special. Everything around here seems to be in perpetual motion through the spirit and activity of the people. A heavy black smoke and steam rises from all sides of the hill and from the distant valleys.[4] Flames appear from large black chimneys. In the distance we can see a coal mine burning, the flames illuminating the sky and surrounding objects. This mine has been burning for years. Water on and water under the bridge. The rage and the terrific groaning of the many steam engines; the knocking, pounding, and other noises of the various machines give one the impression of being in a different world, until you wake up from the dream and find yourself in Pittsburgh where the noise and confusion starts with the unloading of the baggage, which is very irritating. The town is not lighted, but people speak of having gas lights soon. The streets are very badly paved and full of dirt and mud.

May 14. I was wandering through town after seven o'clock. The houses are black from the soot, poorly built, and undescribably dirty. You see many miserable shacks all over town; but the setting is highly romantic. The Allegheny and Monongahela rivers unite here and flow together to become the Ohio River. The town itself lies between the two rivers. On the banks of both rivers are several smaller towns, which also are blackened by coal dust and soot from the furnaces.

---

[4] Today we would call it smog.

16

The ships, most of them steam but designed differently from those one sees in the Atlantic ports, are all anchored mid-stream in the Monongahela not far above the confluence of the two rivers.

Afternoon. On a high hill called Hogsback, opposite Pittsburgh, sits Alleghenytown, its houses also wreathed in smoke and steam. I am standing at the entrance to a seminary, high on the mountain. Before me, in the shape of a triangle, lies the town of Pittsburgh. At my right is the point where the two rivers form the Ohio. From the color of the rivers, one can see clearly how the waters mix. The Allegheny and Monon-gahela are light in color and the beginning of the Ohio is cloudy and dark; otherwise smooth and even as a mirror and therefore called by the Indians "la belle rivière." Two long, covered bridges are before me. Heavy smoke and mist limit the view.

Alleghenytown itself is neat, with small public gardens, the first I have seen in America. Behind me, on the other side of the hill, is a very fertile valley. In the distance to the left are black, wooded mountains beyond which the Ohio flows toward the Mississippi Valley. This afternoon I visited an iron foundry where a steam engine with the power of 110 horses was oper-ating many other machines. Great lumps of molten iron were flattened with terrific noise under giant hammers, then reheated and drawn into long bars. Muscular giants handled the red-hot iron as if they were playing with toys; small boys made nails, or I should say, they operated nail-making machinery. It was a terrific noise—rattling, rolling, hissing, and boiling caused by water, fire, steam, and the red-hot iron. It looked to me like a swarm of subterranean ghouls being released from Hades. I shuddered as I wandered away from this wild scene and was glad when I found myself in the open air again. I visited still another iron foundry where all kinds of machinery were cast; the same noise, fire, and flame all over again.

May 15.   Early in the morning. Coal Hill, a steep, difficult climb opposite Hogsback and on the other side of the Monongahela bridge. From the top of this hill one has a perfect view of the city and the surrounding area to the right. Here can be seen the little town of Birmingham in a picturesque valley created by the Monongahela and surrounded by fertile plantations; in the distance, behind the town, dense forests. From here one can see how both rivers emerge from the hinterland. Grant's Hill is another high point located opposite Coal Hill and at an angle from Birmingham. On the left the Ohio. Everything is shrouded in smoke and steam. The day is friendly, no clouds in the sky.

11 O'Clock.   On board the steamship *Wacousta* on the Monongahela. These steamers have three decks and 20 to 80 staterooms. Down below in the hold is the merchandise, then comes the engine, exposed in the middle of the ship; the remainder of the space is for passengers. On the second deck are the staterooms for ladies and gentlemen, the ship's offices, and various storage compartments. On the third or top deck is the Captain's bridge. The first and second decks are surrounded by railings, but not the third deck, which serves as a promenade in good weather. These river steamers travel to Louisville and St. Louis, and a few of them go as far as New Orleans and return.

10 O'Clock in the Evening. At Wheeling, Virginia, where the steamer anchored, I went ashore. This town, again, is located on a hill. From the boat landing, one goes up a wooden stairs and finds himself in front of the United States Hotel, a neat inn on Water Street. Parallel with Water Street is Main Street. Here I met a German laborer, with whom I conversed regarding his circumstances. He was not satisfied with his position and was very discouraged. According to him, there was no well-to-do German living in Wheeling; yet he spoke of a so-called Herrn von Vogt, a young Prussian, who has lived in Wheeling for several years with no apparent occupation. Recently, Von Vogt married the daughter of a butcher. Two German churches are here, one Catholic and one Evangelical.

Traveling on the Ohio is most comfortable. It is rightly called by the Indians the "Gentle River" because it is flowing gently between beautifully wooded banks. The river winds in a thousand bends through open valleys and narrow gorges. At times one is embraced by the nearness of the mountains;

then suddenly, around the next bend, appears a striking panoramic view. Now and then we pass green islands when the river separates in different channels; then in the background appear the green hills beyond the so-called bottom land, where small villages and individual cabins appear occasionally. Signs of flooding when the river was above its normal level can be seen on both banks. Trees with their roots exposed may be observed here and there. Today we stopped at a little town on the Virginia side to take aboard a load of American emigrants with wives, children, and all their possessions. They did not look very inviting. Their hopes seemed to be pinned on the Far West (wherever Americans live in the West, they believe there are greater opportunities even farther in that direction). So far I have seen no Germans among these emigrants; most of them were Americans from the Eastern states and Irish. I talked with an elderly farmer who was on his way West. He told me all he wanted was to see and embrace his son once more before his death. He seemed to be an honest soul who has lived far from the polluted air of the Atlantic Coast cities.

May 16. Sunrise and we are still at Wheeling. I went ashore again to see the town. It is very quiet except for Water and Main streets. Because of its location, Wheeling is very attractive. Thirty years ago the city was insignificant. From here on, the banks of the Ohio are becoming wilder and more sublime. Dense forests, far-away blue hills, green islands, the rarest color shadings, graceful and fertile areas, especially on the Virginia side. The river bends so often that one sees a change in the air every quarter hour. First it is very windy, even cold, so that a coat is necessary; then suddenly it is mild and friendly; the sun shines on the distant hills, but the river is often in shadow. The Mingoes once lived in this romantic part of the country, but there is no longer any sign of their existence except in legends. Oh, pitiful definition of human beings, what is immortality? I saw several so-called floating stores. These are flat boats. Instead of an upper deck, there is a small wooden house that contains merchandise. With this boat, the owner travels from house to house along the river to offer his wares. One of these floating stores was loaded with pots and chairs. A small white flag, fastened to a long stick, denotes its purpose. Eight miles before Marietta we anchored at the bank of the river to load firewood; this is called "wooding." I entered one of the many farm cabins and met a sixty-year-old farmer, surrounded by his family. Strange! This I would never have believed. The living quarters were poor and shabby, but the farm itself was beautiful to behold. Everything was doing well except the peach trees. He was Irish and had come to this land 40 years ago as a poor man. Now he is a landowner and has saved $14,000; yet he still lives in his primitive dwelling. Nine years ago he bought land here at $9 per acre; four years ago he was offered $25 per acre. Like all Irish, he was a dedicated "Jacksonist" but a man of healthy, strong mind and good common sense, like most American farmers. After five o'clock in the afternoon, while sight-seeing in Marietta, an annoying incident took place. Our steamer left without us, and we had to take after it in a shallop from the Muskingum River and into the Ohio, where the boat waited for us. If we had not had the steward of the boat in our party, we would have been left behind. Or did it happen because many of us, including myself, hadn't paid our fare? Marietta lies above a high bank of the river, on a beautiful plain. It has a few big buildings and is a friendly spot. Somebody offered me a house with a small yard for $1,000. Near Marietta is a three-mile-long island in the Ohio that is known as Blennerhassett. The river's divided channels bend very gracefully around the island. The eye cannot penetrate the dense foliage. In 1806 Vice-President Burr plotted with the Mexican government against the United States. Blennerhassett, owner of the island, was the agent of the conspirators, and here Burr and his associates held their secret meetings. This secluded spot appears to have been the right place for their purposes. Vice-President Burr was tried for conspiracy and, oddly enough, was found not guilty.[5]

Sunday, May 17. We are wooding again. I went ashore to a newly built log cabin. The owner had several acres on lease for which he paid $5 per acre per year. He cuts the wood and sells it to the passing steamers at a dollar and a quarter per cord. This is an advantage to the owner, whose land is being cleared of trees and can be sold later for cultivation. The State of Kentucky begins on our left side at the Big Sandy River. Not far from here, on the Ohio side, stands an iron coffin on a brick pedestal and covered with a white roof which is sup-

---

[5] This isolated piece of land in the Ohio River below the mouth of the Little Kanawha, an Indian rendezvous, was first known as Backus Island. Harman Blennerhassett, an Irishman of obscure origin, purchased the north end of the island in 1798 and built Blennerhassett House where he and Aaron Burr later were alleged to have plotted to commit a treasonable act against the United States. Blennerhassett was imprisoned, but released after Burr was exonerated.

ported by wooden pillars. A rich farmer wished to be buried in this manner on his own land. There he lies now! What capricious notions some human beings have. The peculiar fellow thought that in this way he would gain eternity; or else, like some Indians, he wanted to be buried with his head sticking up above the ground.

Portsmouth — at the mouth of the Scioto. Here we load and unloaded and there was time to go ashore. The little town sits on a high plateau above the valley, against a background of hills and forests. From here there is a canal that connects with Lake Erie. We can see a few large warehouses, also several iron foundries. I talked with a young woman about the canal.

Maysville, Ky., is a town of approximately 3,000 inhabitants. It lies at a bend in the river and the houses appear to be beautiful, even splendid. Three large gilt lanterns can be seen at the river's edge. Across from Maysville is Aberdeen. A ferry boat connects the two banks of the river. Along the Ohio one finds plenty of stores and taverns here. The hills behind both towns are cultivated. The people are coming out of church and they look very European. I wonder if it is not better to live in the wilderness, far from the American civilization, instead of with this mixture of rustic incompleteness. I think that most of the Americans today are repulsive. I feel much happier when I am on the water and can see all the natural beauty of the land.

May 19. At eleven o'clock last night I was awakened by the noise of a gun, and when I reached the deck I found myself in Cincinnati, the "Great Queen of the West." Except for a few lights, the city was in darkness. Arriving and departing steamers made a terrific noise. The steamers on the western rivers are the high-pressure type, much more powerful than those in the East. I went ashore at dawn. This town was founded only 33 years ago, and now it has a population of 33,000.

May 23. At the hotel in Cincinnati. This place is very expensive, inconveniently furnished—even dirty. I couldn't close an eye during my three nights here because of bedbugs and other vermin. From here I moved to another place, even less convenient, but at least free of vermin. What must the Far West be like, if this is the Queen of the West? Everything here is very unsettled and unfinished. The house I am in has no locks on the doors, hardly a table and chair in each room, no mirrors or other conveniences. And what kind of people are found here? What rotten riffraff! It is as if all the jails in the world had been opened. I never would have believed that there were people like this in Germany. In the past two or three years, I am told, the population of this place has increased by eight to nine thousand. They come from the lowest classes and their influence is a bad one. There are hundreds of inns and taverns, known as "coffee houses," and most of them are owned by Germans. One can hardly walk a dozen steps without seeing one of these places. The contrast in living quarters is amazing. There are expensive houses, occupied by wealthy Yankees, and wretched hovels where the foreigners live in miserable poverty. They live, but how? Like vegetables! As in the rest of the country, the main public buildings are churches, which are found in great numbers and of various odd styles. I saw one church that was a mixture of all architectural classifications, even Turkish influence. On Main Street and Broadway are a few handsome private homes. Let us not forget the Trollope Bazaar, which, through *Manners*, written by its founder, has become world famous. The building already is beginning to fall apart, and now in the temple of this exasperated lady one finds only a bar or tavern.[6] The inner rooms are furnished quite tastefully. In Germany, a building of this type that was designed for social entertainment would be very well patronized; but here, where none is interested in social life, the place is dead except for the bar, which is occupied by drunkards. The pillars at the rear of the building are covered with mud, dirt, and coal dust.

May 24. I am so poorly established here that it is difficult to keep up this journal. This afternoon, as I was wandering through the outskirts of town, I thought all at once that I was in a miserable village in Germany. Everywhere Germans of the poorest kind. Here and there I saw a well-to-do vegetable gardener. As in Germany, I see women working in the fields. I talked with several of them and was told that they earn thirty-seven and a half cents a day. I also met a chemist by the

---

[6] In his *Cities of America*, George S. Perry stated that Mrs. Frances Trollope opened her bazaar in Cincinnati in 1828, stocked with goods bought from local merchants at retail prices, marked up, and offered for resale. The enterprise was unsuccessful and Mrs. Trollope returned to her native land where, in 1832, at Harrow, she published a caustic two-volume work, *Domestic Manners of the Americans*. It was widely read and highly praised for its literary merit although greatly resented by Americans. An American edition was published in New York in 1894.

name of Homburg who recently came back from Arkansas.
He told me of the German colonies that attempted to settle
there. He, himself, belonged to a group of several hundred
people who landed at New Orleans, went up the Mississippi
and Red rivers to Little Rock. After a brief stay in Little Rock,
they moved on to find suitable land for permanent settlement.
There was disagreement over the condition of the land because each farmer considered only personal interests. Moving
farther up the Red River, the colony finally reached the selected spot, which was little more than a jungle. The first and
most important building to be erected is the blockhouse,
for protection against the weather. They started to cut trees
for the blockhouse, only to be told by their American neighbors that they had cut the wrong type of tree and that the
blockhouse would last only a few months. Furthermore, they
discovered that the axes brought from Germany were useless
with this kind of forest. They had to give up building the blockhouse themselves and hire American laborers whom they paid
a dollar and a quarter per day. And so their first house cost
them $60. After they moved into it, and the land was divided
among the members of the colony, they started to clear the
trees. Although they were used to hard labor all their lives, they
spent the whole day cutting one tree. Unlucky as they were, the
rainy season began, and many of them became ill from ex-
posure to the elements. After many days of rain, the river
flooded the colony. They were completely isolated from their
neighbors and were without food and other necessities. It was

decided by lot who would swim the river to get help. Many drowned. The survivors abandoned the site, some going back to New Orleans and others to Cincinnati. This was one of the many abortive efforts to find a new Germany!!

May 25. Yesterday, Sunday, I went with several German people to the so-called Pleasure Garden, which is owned by a German, the Americanized Mr. Rice. Before I reached my destination I felt as though I were in Germany; nothing but Germans and more Germans. I am sorry to say they were from the meanest and toughest class of people. They wore their outlandish German outfits. One seldom sees an American on Sunday. They remain in their churches to beguile the time. Arriving at the Garden, one stops in front of a small wooden house where I bought two tickets, which cost 12 1/2 cents each. The barroom is very crowded with people, both drunk and sober. They argue and fight until a constable arrives to restore order. You should hear the way they murder the English language. One would think the Goddess of Liberty holds full sway here because of the roughness and licentiousness of the people. The cultivated man leaves this temple of wickedness to breathe the clean air. The garden itself is large and has many flowers, arranged in the typical American way. Despite huge signs warning the people to keep off the flowers, they trample and break them. Nowhere is there any shade. Here and there are boxes and benches for people to sit. All one hears is common talk, rough, vulgar language. Meanness and vulgarity reign supreme. The only refreshments available are beer and spirits, mixed in the American fashion, and a few cakes. Everything is very poor and dirty. The waiters are the meanest and toughest of ruffians. They answer you in a drawling Y-e-e-e-s and N-o-o-o. Curiosity satisfied, one is only too happy to leave this vulgar atmosphere and breathe freely again.

May 27. Last night I attended a meeting at the Wesley Methodist Church to establish a new political group named the Emigrants Friends Society. The increase in the number of emigrants, particularly from Germany and Ireland, has caused apprehension among the cultivated Americans for some time. This situation is discussed in the newspapers as being very disadvantageous to the institutions of the country. There are two political parties—the Democrats and the Whigs. The former has been dominant since the Presidency of Andrew Jackson because it represents the masses and the rabble. This party will do anything to attain its objectives. On the other hand, the Whigs are made up of the cultivated and the wealthy citizens. The Democratic party tries to humiliate the Whigs and to lure the higher class of people by deceit, intrigue, and trickery into the party. By violating the election laws and bypassing the naturalization laws under which emigrants attain citizenship, the Democratic party is increasing by thousands every year. Most of them come from the lowest classes in Europe. Intellectually they are incapable of understanding the Constitution and the laws of the United States. This mound of European excrement is used by the Democratic party to increase its strength. The other party is smart enough to realize the serious threat to the Republic and is trying by education and explanation to stop the growth of the Democratic party. For this reason the Emigrant Friends Society was formed. They plan to build schools for educating children of emigrants in order that they may become useful members of the state. They have a long way to go to achieve their goal. The biggest problem is the financial one. Money must be raised by private contribution. Professors and clerics addressed the meeting, appealing for funds. Professor Stowe, in particular, spoke very effectively about the dangers of the political situation and what can be done to correct it. After the speeches, an attempt was made to collect money. From what I saw, it was not much. Except for a few pork dealers, there are not many wealthy people in this town. They have the necessities of life, but they don't appreciate what they have.

May 29. Today I moved into the third apartment since I arrived here. Except for a few private houses, everything is shabby and dirty. The landlords are people who cover their meanness with religion. They quote a price of two and a half dollars per week in a boardinghouse, but before the week is over they raise the price to two and three quarters. They have no character. Money is their only objective. Inexperienced foreigners are cheated at every turn. They have no friendship, hospitality, or respect for anybody. One finds no friends of nature, only ruffians and libertines.

June 15. During the three weeks of my stay on the beautiful banks of the Ohio River I have had very little to write about. After one has seen the surroundings there isn't much more to say about the American way of life because it is the same everywhere. The people in the West are more primitive than in the East. Yesterday I went with W for a boat ride on the Licking River. It is quite a nice river, both banks being still in their original state of wildness from Indian times. Huge maple trees hang over the water, and in the distance one sees thick forests and black hills. The forests mark the course of the river. Vines, thick as my arm, embrace the trees and hang down into the water. We went ashore on the left bank to visit a five-acre farm that formerly belonged to a Frenchman, who planted European willows along the river. We saw several unusual trees, one in particular with large thorns. On our way back it began to grow dark. A fisherman encouraged us to buy his entire catch—five big catfish—which he said he would sell to us for a quarter of a dollar. It was night when we reached the Ohio.

June 17. Made an excursion in the company of a land-scape painter from Mühlhausen. We went east over the canal bridge, then left by the water works, and climbed up a steep mountain, on the top of which we visited an Irish dairy farmer. This man was very talkative and hospitable. When he learned that we were Europeans, he invited us into his cabin, but when he told us that two of his boys were "sick of a little touch of cholera morbus" we fled. After drinking some milk, we sat down on the grass and inspected the landscape. Marvelous and charming! Civilization mixed with the wild, romantic scenery. To the right of the town is the fertile valley. The winding main street runs toward Columbus. At the left the soft, streaming Ohio and the mouth of the little Licking. On both sides of the latter, one sees the charming little towns of Newport and Covington, with the Ohio stretching beyond, thick forests on either side, and here and there a cabin. One must see the region to appreciate its beauty. On our way back we visited the Schnelz Garden. Mr. Martin Schnelz is a German who built a small but quite attractive botanical garden on a parcel of land near the canal. A clear well provides fresh, clean water—the only fresh water in Cincinnati. Everywhere is river water, which is muddy, and when it rains it is extremely disgusting to drink. The well is deep and is located in a sort of cave or grotto, decorated with beautiful flowers and shrubs. It shows great taste and sense of artistic arrangement. It is an amusement park where one can obtain refreshment. I used to go here quite often, but seldom did I meet anyone. Mr. Schnelz also has an aviary in his garden where he raises canaries. He travels with his birds and plants a great deal because he makes very little money at home.

June 23. Newport Mineral Wells. That sounds very well and one expects something like Wiesbaden or Bad Schwalbach, or perhaps even an American Baden Baden! But no! From Newport, beyond Cincinnati, one goes a little to the left over a hill and through a few mountain ravines until one is on top of a small green observation point where there is a beautiful view of Cincinnati. To the left is a little brook that is completely dry in summertime, and thence the road runs through a series of hills and valleys, thinly wooded. From the observation point one sees a long, wooden, cheaply built house. The numbered rooms extend to the right and left from the hall on one floor only. In the center of the structure is the ever-present barroom. Alongside this house is a similar building with one large hall and several partitions for the ladies. The first thing a European would ask is: "Where are the baths?" But where are they? They show you a common well with a bucket on a rope, offering nothing better than bad well water. The only advantage of the place is that it is quite high and isolated. It has clean, fresh mountain air. It could be a very pleasant spot for rest and recreation, but the Americans have no appreciation of the beauties of nature, and therefore an establishment of this kind enjoys no popularity. All establishments of this kind are little more than common inns. We were there on a Sunday afternoon, and there were hardly ten patrons, including ourselves. This public bath, if it can be called such, seems to exist only from the income of the tavern or bar. The German type of mineral baths will never succeed in this country unless the Americans find a need for relaxation and recreation. Most of the Germans in America cannot afford such luxuries.

Military Station on the Licking

At the mouth of the Licking River on the Newport side stands a beautiful white wooden house where, on a high wooden pole, the American flag flies. Here one finds the military station of 15 to 20 men, a few drummers, one fife, a trumpet, and a bass drum. Since the American ground force is used for the sole purpose of protection against Indians, one wonders how the military happens to be here, hundreds of miles from the frontier, and there is nothing to fear from enemy devastation. It is also far from the Atlantic Coast and the French-Canadian border. What is the reason for such a large force here? No other reason than to recruit the men from nearby towns and farms. They want to impress the people with the glamour of military life. They hired recruits for five years because they wanted to send them to the Far West where they died of disease. This bothered me because I lived just across from the barracks and had to listen almost all day to the disgusting drumming, whistling, bass drumming, and trumpet sounds. This noisy unmilitary group of musicians, led by a noncommissioned officer with a shiny sword in his fist, marches through the town by day, accompanied by hundreds of cheering, noisy boys and drunkards. At times that constant drumming across from me continued until late at night. I could hardly stand it. Sometimes I thought they even made the music in their sleep.

June 24. The Museum of the Infernal Regions. When one speaks of a museum in this country, it is not the same as the European museum. Here in the land of liberty art institutes are not founded by the state, but rather by private individuals and

organizations for profit, catering to the popular taste. All big
cities in America, where the people are of the lower class, have
many such institutions. They are big buildings with large rooms
where all kinds of curios are displayed, such as wax figures,
mammoth bones, skeletons, skulls, sea shells, stones, stuffed
birds, and Indian relics. Huge billboards with giant letters, illuminated at night, attract public attention. Even raucous
music is used for the same purpose. Even here in the Queen of
the West, these enticements alone are not enough to arouse the
curiosity of the people. One proprietor, Mr. D'Orville, was
very successful in arousing the curiosity of the western Republicans and became wealthy. Listen! A man named Power, a
cunning Yankee with an understanding of mechanical engineer-
ing and crude sculpture constructed a Hell with life-sized devils
where sinners were burned by fire and flame. I was in a lower
room of this museum where ladies amused themselves by looking at peep shows and gentlemen were banging a bass drum
when suddenly a small bell rang and a boy announced in a loud
voice: "Ladies and Gentlemen, the infernal regions are ready."
Head over heels, everybody ran out of the room through a small
door that led over a small stair well into a dark room. Here, one
is separated by a wood railing from the horrible caves where the
devils live and here they tell us we are in Hell. To the left is a
deep cave from which a rattlesnake escapes. In front of this cave
is a huge dog that snaps at a naked sinner, trying to pull the
flesh from his body. At the right stands Beelzebub, who makes
the most revolting grimaces while answering questions from the

audience. High in the center hangs a criminal on the gallows. A waxen figure of a woman is dragged, screaming, into a cave to be burned in sulphur flames. There are many other scenes, but they are too distasteful to describe. All these activities are accompanied by horrible creaking, groaning, and whistling. Suddenly, one feels a terrible electric shock, the lights are extinguished, and we are in total darkness. Then follow a terrific rattling, hissing, and whining that cause chills up and down the spine. One must have strong nerves to keep from fainting. After a period of complete silence, the lights return and one sees the terrified faces of the women. The ministers think that this show has a salutary effect on people, and Mr. D'Orville feels it causes people to grow closer to religion and to give more money to the church.

July 1. The day before yesterday, Sunday, I walked upstream along the bank of the river. I went to Mill Creek, where the countryside is more picturesque. There were beautiful country homes on the hillsides and along the river all the way to the Four Mile Resort, a park where the Cincinnati people go for refreshment and to enjoy the view. It was a beautiful day, but I saw very few people. The grounds, which extend to the riverbank, contain a garden and a white stone house. At the river is a small bench. The garden is small and poorly arranged, like most American gardens. The refreshments were all alcoholic, except at strawberry time, when it is fashionable for the ladies to eat strawberry cream. One cannot find social entertainment such as music and dancing because it doesn't exist in this place. After we had a few bottles of beer, for which we paid 18 3/4 cents per bottle, we returned home, a ten-mile walk.

The Females of Cincinnati

I do not know why, but the women of the eastern states, particularly the women of Philadelphia, have exceptional faces. Is it the climate, the way of living, or religion that so mysteriously influences the females of this country? One of these unknown factors must be responsible for the ugliness of their faces and figures. One walks through the streets, visits the churches, or meets them at the stores where they do their daily shopping. Everywhere one meets those long, pale, distorted faces, plump bodies, and thick ankles. One German called them "Calomel Faces," which is very appropriate when you consider how much of this poison they consume, on advice of the American doctors, from childhood to the grave. The climate also takes its toll of the weaker sex. Were they not dressed in such bright colors, one would think they are burdened with grief or other misfortune. In my opinion, their appearance is caused by the monotony of their daily lives. Their eyes are dull and spiritless. They appear to lack interest in cultural things like art and science. There is no smile on their lips or friendly glance in their eyes. Their demeanor is morose, cold, and peevish. Such is the so-called beautiful sex.

July 2. It was so cold all night that even with doors and windows closed, one couldn't get warm in bed. The quick changes in the weather cause illness, no matter how strong you may be. Today is so hot that one suffocates, there is no breeze, you perspire and pant for breath under the burning sun. One discards heavy clothes and gets into linens, when suddenly there is a storm, accompanied by thunder and lightning. The following day can be cold enough for furs. Such rapid climatic changes cause much illness. For this reason, many Europeans lose their health and enterprise in the New World.

July 8. Trip from Cincinnati to the Wabash River. About 8 o'clock in the evening I left Cincinnati aboard the steamship *Indian.* Since the Wabash River is very shallow, shallow-draft boats are necessary. Cabins for ladies are upstairs and for gentlemen, downstairs. Despite limited space, the cabins are very conveniently arranged. The captain, a Scotsman by birth, is very friendly and helpful, which is seldom the case with American captains. The ship's clerk collects the fares and the captain is interested only in operating the ship. He has the honor to sit at the head of the table at meal time. This practice should be suggested to the American captains.

July 9. The banks of the Ohio become wilder, the villages and plantations less frequent as we approach the mouth of the river. One sees nothing but hills, covered by thick forests. Two o'clock—the view toward the town of Louisville, Kentucky. The Ohio becomes wider, the banks more flat, now only thinly forested. The town is built at a bend of the river. It looks

as if it were stemming the flow of water. In the far distance is
a long blue strip of high forest, which gives the town a colorful
background. But how different in the foreground! In one
and a half hours I wandered through the entire town, which
claims 15,000 inhabitants. The streets are long and wide, but
dirty, with only a few nice houses and many huts. One feels the
presence of a slave state. Main Street is the prettiest. Then
Jefferson and Market. The largest and best-looking building in
town is the Louisville Hotel on Main Street. Along Front
Street, near the river, are big stores and even bigger cafés, as
in Cincinnati. The cheapest cafés are owned by Germans
of the lowest class. There were 12 steamboats anchored in the
river. During the season, Louisville is engaged in considerable
trade with Indiana and its other neighboring states. The town
is built on a plain. On the far side are new streets under construction, the workers being Germans and colored slaves who
work together under the same overseer. Except for Main Street
and the water front, everything was dead and deserted. As one
travels farther west, things become less secure and more warlike,
the people carrying long knives and guns, with powder horns
slung at their sides. Aboard ship they constantly practice shoot-
ing. Some with no shoes on their feet are carrying guns worth
$20 to $30.

July 10.   Until this morning we anchored at the entrance to the canal for loading and unloading of cargo. Here,
where the Ohio is quite broad, are the so-called rapids: a group

of rocks through which the river drops 60 feet. Boats can pass the rapids only at high water; otherwise they must unload their cargoes, which is a great hindrance to trade. Someone got the idea of bypassing the rapids with a three-mile canal, which runs on the Kentucky side of the river through rocky terrain. The banks of the canal are reinforced by levies made of the surplus rock. Before the canal returns to the river we must pass through several locks, some of which are 30 feet high. Over each lock is a stone bridge and while we were passing through one lock, the bridge was crossed by a carriage on its way to Shippingport, a small place with a big café. This canal cost more than two million dollars. On the other hand, the canal makes money by collecting a toll of $20 to $200, depending upon the tonnage of the boat. Too bad this canal is not wide enough for boats to pass each other. At the mouth of the canal the river has a current of between 5 and 6 miles per hour, caused by the rapids. Opposite Louisville is Jeffersonville, Indiana, and not far from the mouth of the canal is New Albany, also in Indiana, a nice town where many steamboats are built and repaired.

Evening. All day long through thick, black forests. Here and there small but very attractive log houses. The beautiful little towns one saw in Ohio have completely disappeared or are seen in embryo. For instance, Fredonia, Indiana, marked in big letters on the map, is only three or four houses and a sawmill. How isolated are the people who live here! While we loaded wood at Fredonia, I climbed the riverbank to a nearby hut in a small clearing in the forest. A woman who looked very poor and sickly disappeared behind the fence after I started to question her. I climbed over the fence and found a dog and a cat in front of the cabin door. At the sight of a strange face, the dog, the cat, and the children disappeared. The owner was a woodchopper who sold wood to the passing boats.

July 11. From 5 o'clock in the morning at Rockport until nightfall we saw nothing but flat riverbanks covered with heavy woods. Hills and mountains have completely disappeared. At Evansville, Indiana, a town of 600—800 people, I went ashore. A few brick houses lined the bank, together with a dry-goods and a boot store. The remainder of the town did not look very inviting. Here I saw several huge floating docks marked "Free Wharf," which were very convenient because of the steep, muddy banks and shallow water. The free wharves float out to the boats, if necessary, to facilitate loading and unloading. Toward evening we saw two peculiar bends in the river. At one the river widened on both sides with a high island in the middle. In passing this island, one has the impression of being on a large lake. After passing the island and looking back, it resembled a large triangle, and for this reason it is called Diamond Island. It is unbelievably symmetrical, with sharp corners and straight sides.

July 12. Last night about 11 o'clock, at the mouth of the Wabash. This river rises in the northwestern part of Ohio and forms the border between the states of Indiana and Illinois and is navigable as far up as Terre Haute and even to Lafayette. Throughout the night I was bothered terribly by swarms of mosquitoes. Nets were placed over the cots to protect us from bites and the buzzing noise. At sunrise we entered the Wabash River and at six o'clock I went ashore. I visited a farmer in the midst of the forest. He had bought 160 acres of land the previous year and so far only seven acres have been cleared for cultivation. The soil appeared to me to be quite rich. A short distance from his abode, where the jungle is still growing, stood his log cabin with three big dogs in front of it. House and farm tools lay all around. A tall, thin, ragged woman, with four half-naked children, one still at her breast, sat before a fire preparing breakfast. The door was open and I entered. The inside of the cabin was not very inviting. The walls had many holes and at the left was a large hearth with a chimney made of tree trunks that appeared to be leaning against the cabin. A cradle, two dirty old-fashioned bedsteads, a long gun, and six to eight plates and a few pots on top of a shelf completed the whole picture of this backwoods family. I intended to visit another log cabin, but when I approached the door I was attacked by four big dogs. An ugly witch held them back. When I asked her why they had so many dogs, she said they were to keep off the wild varmints. Much of the land along the Illinois side of the Wabash River is Congress land and for sale at $1.25 per acre. Doubtless it will remain in Government ownership a long time, because overflow from the river makes cultivation impossible. The woods are like thick jungles, with large trees and huge wild grape vines as big as a man's body. Passage through these woods is impossible because of the vines. On account of the annual floods, the soil is very loose. Six to eight feet above ground the trees are marked by the water at flood level. On both sides the riverbanks are steep and hard to climb. When one sets foot on the wet soil he is attacked by millions of mosquitoes.

July 13. Because of the so-called bars when, in summertime, the Wabash has only a few feet of water, we had to stop to unload the freight on a lighter, which the boat has carried for that purpose. This took all day yesterday and last night, until about five o'clock this morning we could proceed. I was bothered badly all night by mosquitoes and other insects. This river, like the Ohio, has remarkable bends around which at low water, as right now, navigation is very difficult. Today we saw one of the most beautiful parts of the river, called Black's Cutoff. The river divides in two parts and forms an island six miles in length. The view at this spot is too beautiful to describe—one must see it with his own eyes.

July 14. We have traveled only 45 miles up the Wabash. Someone has just tossed an anchor toward a point of land where the river makes a sharp bend.

July 15. Finally, near ten o'clock, we could proceed. It took us all day yesterday to pass a new bar near New Harmony.[7] The farmers from the surrounding country had to help us. An

---

[7] George Rapp, the German separatist, and his followers from Württemberg had founded the community of Economy, Pennsylvania, and had moved to Harmony, Indiana, in 1814. When the property was sold to Robert Owen they returned to Economy, leaving behind them on the 20,000 acres of partially cleared land no less than 180 brick, frame, and log buildings, including shops, factories, community facilities, and housing for approximately seven hundred people. Robert Owen, English-born textile manufacturer who developed a social theory popularly known as Owenism, sought to understand and control the great forces that were influencing the early nineteenth-century English society by becoming first a social reformer and later an advocate of communitarian socialism. By 1817 he had acquired national stature in England as a

engine broke down, and someone had to go ashore a few miles to find a blacksmith who could repair the damage. After sundown we arrived at New Harmony, a small town of 600 inhabitants, most of them Americans. Six years ago a man named Rapp and his company of settlers turned over the location of the town to an Englishman named Owen. Rapp went to the town of Economy on the Ohio River. After his community property plan failed, Owen sold the land to an American and returned to England. The settlement has not grown since because the inhabitants who remained and clung to Owen's religious views are disliked by the Americans, who call them atheists. This is supposed to be the main reason why the settlement, with its beautiful farms and well-kept acres, came to a standstill. The German church of Rapp's time can still be seen, but instead of religious services, the people hold dances there. Here, as everywhere along the Wabash, one can see signs of the annual flood, and for this reason there is still a lot of Congress land. Only here and there, on the highest banks, one sees log cabins. The river, which today offered many of its beauties, also displayed signs of its capricious nature in the form of swift rapids and large tree trunks on the sand bars. Each year, because of the terrific current at flood stage, the river has new bends, islands, and channels.

July 18. Written in the house of Mr. Flower, founder of the colony and the town of Albion.[8] On July 15th at 10 o'clock in the morning we arrived at Grayville which, like many

---

social reformer, but his theories became controversial during the next seven years, and for this reason, in 1824, he crossed the Atlantic for the purpose of inspecting the site of the Rapp colony in southern Indiana.

According to Arthur Eugene Bestor, in *Backwoods Utopias* (Philadelphia, 1950) 49n, Owen's interest in the Rapp property was solicited by Richard Flower, father of George Flower who, with Morris Birkbeck, had founded the English immigrant community of Albion, a few miles north of Harmony on the Illinois side of the Wabash in 1817–1818. Owen bought the Rapp property intact in January, 1825, and renamed it New Harmony. The purchase price is believed to have been $125,000. Steven Stone, former New England ship-owner and blockade runner, is credited with negotiating the sale (*Charter No.*

other little towns, cannot be found on the map of the United States. It is located at the mouth of the Bon-Pas Creek, a small stream that runs into the Wabash River. This town was founded five years ago by a gentleman named Gray, who has established a store in a settlement comprising two stores, six to eight small log cabins, and a blacksmith shop. From here I intended traveling to Albion, but couldn't get a carriage of any kind to complete the journey. Nor was there an inn where I could stay at Grayville. If a farmer had not taken me in for money and good words, I would have had to spend the night in the open air. I remained with several other immigrants, all English, who had their wives and children with them, in this hut. Space was very limited, and we stayed all in one room. On account of my glasses, the farmer thought I was a doctor and gave me the preference of a bed, in which I spent a sleepless night. At dawn I piled my belongings on a wagon drawn by four oxen belonging to a farmer who lived a few miles from Albion. My English traveling companions were going to work for him. Four miles from Albion I met a Kentuckian of German descent who took me in his carriage, pulled by two horses, to Albion for a dollar. At Albion I stayed in a tavern owned by an Englishwoman, Mrs. Wood.

After lunch I went to see Mr. Flower, who greeted me most cordially and invited me to his farm a few miles from town for the duration of my visit in Albion. I accepted his offer. Late at night I had an accident that could have ended very unhappily. I was riding in a small carriage, accompanied by a young Eng-

---

176: A Short History of the First National Bank of Peoria, Illinois 1863–1963, 8.) His son William E. Stone, cashier and the bank's first president, married Gertrude, daughter of Harriet and Frederick Julius Gustorf. Their children were William Edward, Jr., Caroline, Frederick, Gertrude, Pauline K., Harry C., and Ethel.

8 George Flower's nonsectarian colony for English artisans is mentioned in preceding note. The community of Wanborough was founded later by Birkbeck, after he and Flower had a disagreement, but it did not long survive the death of its founder. Birkbeck, a former tenant farmer in England, stimulated immigration from his native land by his *Notes on a Journey in America*. First published in 1817, it went through eleven editions. *Letters from Illinois*,

lishman who had settled in Peoria and was in Albion for a visit. We returned to town in order to fetch my suitcase. It was very dark, the road was bad through the woods. One of the horses became frightened and ran away. My driver fell out of the carriage and under the horses. I tried to grab the reins, but fell sidewise into the mud. At this moment the horses, fortunately, became tangled in the bushes and came to a standstill. If this hadn't happened, my companion, who was holding onto the tongue of the vehicle, would have broken every bone in his body. Both of us escaped with only a few bruises. We unhitched the horses and walked them home, leaving the carriage to be recovered later by the laborers.

September 4. In the tavern of the old Mrs. Wood in Albion. A long intermission in my diary while I collected practical experience in farming. The American farming system is not as simple as it is described in German and other European publications. Over here the individual farmer does not have to work as hard as the peasant class in Europe, where the whole family has to help make a living. For these people, farming as it is practiced in the western states would be Paradise as compared with farming in Europe. The occupation of farming is almost impossible for an immigrant in this country, especially one who is physically unfit for this kind of work and therefore dependent upon others for help. He would be foolhardy, because it would lead to nothing in the long run, as experience has demonstrated in many cases.

published a year later, reached seven editions and was translated into French and German. Probably Birkbeck's greatest contribution to early Illinois history was his opposition to the introduction of slavery into the state and his support of Illinois's second governor, Edward Coles, who also opposed slavery. Under the pseudonym of Jonathan Freeman, Birkbeck wrote a series of letters pointing out the evils of slavery and denying that slave labor would increase land values. After the slavery referendum was rejected, proslavery members of the Illinois senate retaliated by refusing to approve Governor Coles's nominees for appointive offices, including Birkbeck as secretary of state. *Journal of the Illinois State Historical Society*, LXI, No. 2 (Summer, 1968), 157–60.

During the harvest season I worked for a farmer without pay. For this purpose I had made for myself several sets of working clothes out of rough linen and mingled with laborers in the hayfields. In the beginning, I worked only two hours daily, one hour in the morning and one in the afternoon. I did the easiest work: raking hay. Easy as the work was, the burning sun was intolerable. The thermometer rose to 100 and over. After an hour's work I was completely soaked with perspiration. I had to change my clothes several times daily. Other kinds of work that I was able to do were: turning the swath with a wooden fork; then when it was dry, to cock it; piling up the hay; loading it on the wagon; then unloading the wagon onto the haystacks. Stacking the hay with an iron fork is very tiring, and even if one works without a shirt and drinks water constantly, it is almost unbearable.[9] These jobs are nothing compared with mowing, ploughing, thinning Indian corn, and grubbing; also cocking oats in stubbly fields. It is almost impossible for someone who is not used to this kind of work from his youth, to handle the scythe, the plough, and the axe to advantage. Americans know best how to swing the axe.

To thin corn, you first have to pull out the weeds, which are one to five feet high, with your bare hands; then you have to pull up the stalks that are too close together so that only three stalks, or five at the most, remain together. After a steady rain, when the rich soil is soaking wet, this is hard work, particularly when you have to keep up with the other laborers. Grubbing means pulling out all plants, bushes, and small trees by the roots in

---

[9] This statement, together with the comments upon the difficulties of farming that follow, is significant in view of the fact that the writer was destined to become a prairie farmer after his marriage.

46

order to clear the ground. For this work one uses a particular kind of axe, shaped like a scythe and fastened to a long stick. This brush prefers to grow over fences, and in a few years it looks like a small forest. There are many kinds of trees, including wild plum, nut, cherry, and apple. Nothing is safe from the grubbing axe, and often the most beautiful and fruitful little trees have to be destroyed to protect the fences from decay and to expand the cultivated areas.

Also, it is very important to know how to handle animals like horses, cattle, pigs, and sheep, because without them a farm is unthinkable. To raise sheep requires special knowledge and years of experience; and even then, there are many hazards for the sheep in the form of diseases and the wolves, which attack at night. I can remember that one night, when I was bothered by the heat and all kinds of bugs in my room, and all the hall doors were open, I was awakened by the terrifying howling of wolves and dogs. Five or six dogs were chasing through the house. A Negress came from the next cabin and woke up the owner with the words: "Master, the wolves must have got amongst the sheep, for they are all scampering about." All in the house jumped up, got their shotguns, and arrived at the pens to find the sheep unharmed.

But back to the main point! Whoever wants to become a farmer in the western states and is unable to do the hard work himself, has to hire laborers with money and good words, which is always difficult and sometimes impossible. Among 100 laborers, you might find one whose work is satisfactory. A farmer who cannot do the heavy work himself must have at least one hired man at a cost of $120 to $170 per year. The main problem is at harvest time, when help is hard to find. The average daily wage is a dollar to a dollar and a half per day plus board.[10] Since help is so hard to find, the American farmers help each other in building their log houses. Prices of farm products are low compared to the cost of farming.

A farmer's life is neither romantic nor idyllic; just hard work with small rewards. A person who has not tried it has no idea what problems are involved. The smallest farm is about 40 acres. Many Americans have 100 acres, some even a thousand. Most of the land on the 40-acre farms is already cleared, ready for cultivation. A 40-acre farm with improvements costs between $250 and $300. The so-called improvements consist of fences around the cleared land, a log cabin, and a shed or shelter for equipment. The log cabin consists of a single room in which the whole family lives, with a big hearth for cooking and heating. Food is very plain—nothing but coffee, tea, bacon, potatoes, and corn bread year-round. Luxury items are cooked apples or wild plums and whiskey mixed with water. Clothing is very poor, made out of home-spun cotton materials. Boots—none, except in the coldest weather; otherwise, everyone goes barefoot.

Most of the settlers who came here in the year 1819 are Englishmen by the names of Flower, Birkbeck, Pickering, Bridges, Clark, and others. Most of them spent all their money to buy their farms. Formerly well-to-do, they now have much land and no buyers. With only one exception, a man named Applegarth

---

[10] Eighty-five years later a great-grandson, at age sixteen, worked as a hired hand on a Vermont dairy farm for a brief summer period at the rate of one dollar a day plus board and room. Needless to say, the experience was just as frustrating as that of his ancestor.

48

[*sic*], all I hear are complaints. Some people try to appear well off and well satisfied in order to make a good impression on the newcomers. An alert observer soon realizes their circumstances and feels sorry for them.

However, things are different with the people who came here from Europe and who lived over there in poverty. As soon as they arrive, father, mother, sons, and daughters can find work and within a year or so can buy Congress land with their savings. I have visited several farmers in this class, and all of them had plenty to eat and drink. A few of them are well-to-do, considering their former circumstances. At home they were dependent laborers. Here, they are independent landowners, living better than most of the better class of settlers, who look upon them with envy. These former Europeans are *"the true democrats!"* — exercising the greatest political influence.

September 6.   Yesterday, between 4 and 5 o'clock in the afternoon, we felt an earthquake. It was quite a sensation. I was sitting in the hall when a strange roaring was heard above us. It happened so fast, we thought something heavy on the upper floor had fallen. All the tenants came running, asking each other: "Did you hear the strange noise? Oh, God, it was an earthquake!" This was nothing new to a few of the tenants. I learned today that the quake was felt in the whole settlement, particularly strong in the fields. The weather yesterday was windy in the morning, cloudy, and later very sultry. After the earth movement, the sky darkened, and about 9 o'clock in the evening we had a thunderstorm with lightning and heavy rain. This morning it is likely to rain and quite cool.

Diseases of the West and the Nature of Pharmaceuticals

The diseases that make their appearance each year after harvest time are very saddening and discouraging to the farmer. Fever and ague (known in Europe as gall bladder fever) are the most common ailments. Most of the patients get their treatment from all kinds of medical bunglers. Few people escape fever and ague, but it is more prevalent among the working classes. Those whose bodies are not exposed to the heat of the sun in summer, who enjoy a varied diet, and who wash themselves frequently are not affected by these diseases. One can estimate the extent of disease in this country by visiting the log cabins, the doctors' offices, and the country stores. According to the people, this county is not as bad as the neighboring counties, since no one wants to admit the presence of disease. In one log cabin I visited, a woman was in bed, sighing and groaning. When I asked what was the matter with her, I was told she had ague. In another cabin, father and children were stricken. In a third cabin the inhabitants were walking around like ghosts: faint, flabby, and enfeebled. What's the matter? I asked. The reply: A chill or a "shake." In [Joel] Churchill's store, where the clerk also serves as pharmacist, they sell quinine, calomel, castor oil, laudanum, and camphor dissolved in alcohol to the sick in great quantities. The doctors (the local doctor is named [Archibald] Spring) are not as well trained as German physicians. They ride around the county on horseback, visiting patients. Very often the patient will send an emissary to Doctor Spring to ask what can be done. When riding horseback the doctors carry medicine in a leather bag, which they throw over the saddle. With the afore-mentioned drugs the doctors cure all diseases. The doctor feels the pulse with a significant expression on his face, then opens his bag and shakes a certain amount of medicine on a little piece of paper. This procedure is repeated with every patient. These and other diseases, unknown to me heretofore, are prevalent along the Mississippi, Missouri, and Illinois rivers, and in the bottom land. Albion, which is 16 miles from the great Wabash, is healthier than the western counties.

September 10. Wanborough. This spot, two to three miles from Albion, was founded by Birkbeck after he and Flower had a disagreement. Like Albion, it is deteriorating. Here are eight or ten dilapidated huts, a mill, a workshop, and a pottery. The soil is supposed to be better here than around Albion, but at this time of year nearly all the residents were sick with the afore-mentioned diseases. All I saw was sad faces. Not far from here, on the western side of the Boltenhouse Prairie, was Birkbeck's country home, a plantation of four to five hundred acres that now lies deserted. During the lifetime of its founder, this settlement is supposed to have been magnificent; but now the land is covered with high weeds, part of the house is torn down, and the remainder is near collapse. The land, which by nature is very productive, with a charming view of the prairie, belongs now to a merchant in New Orleans who has tried for two years to sell it for $1.25 per acre. It includes a beautiful orchard, where the most delicious apples and plums lie on the ground in heaps under the trees. I took a handkerchiefful home with me. They have no worth because of overabundance.

Birkbeck himself drowned a few years ago in the Fox River when he tried to cross it on horseback. Since his death, his sons and daughters have scattered and those people who knew Birkbeck have only a faint memory of him.

September 12. The prairies. Near Albion are several prairies known as Boltenhouse, Village, Long, and Burned prairies. On the Boltenhouse Prairie are only English farmers, the original settlers. Here are to be seen the most beautiful farms. The other prairies, particularly Village and Long, are owned by Americans from Kentucky and Tennessee. I prefer the Village Prairie, partly because of its charming and romantic location and also because its land is still being sold at the government price. A man named Wiggins in Cincinnati bought five to six hundred acres under tax title and is reselling it at 37 1/2 cents per acre. The prairies in this state are charming—great stretches of flat land, covered with wild meadows that are hemmed by thin forests. The prairies are covered all summer long with flowers that change color every month—yellow, blue, then red. By wandering from one meadow to another, one encounters a series of surprises. Huge green surfaces of unbelievably high grass that waves in the wind like the sea, against a wooded background, more beautiful than the English parks described by Piehler Moskau.

These prairies are from ten to 100 miles across. Because of their size, one can travel over them by horse only. It is enchanting when you come to a little stream in the forest, where the horse can have a drink of water. Then you ride through the small wood and emerge on the other side on another wide expanse of prairie. In winter, when the trails are covered with snow, people get lost and cannot find shelter. I have heard of instances when travelers, lost in the snow on the prairies, have had to slit the bellies of their horses for the warmth of their bodies. In summer, the prairie insects are so numerous that the horses are often stung to death by them. Therefore, one must travel during the night or the early morning hours. Flies settle by the thousands on the horses, and after a ride of several hours, the blood can be seen trickling down their sides. To get relief from these pests, a horse will break into a fast gallop.

September 15.   I had a wonderful opportunity, through the acquaintance of Doctor Spring, to visit settlers in all directions while he visited his patients. Today we took a ride of ten miles over the Village, Bonpas, Buck, and Mill prairies. On the latter we visited a farm where, in a small, miserable cabin, a family has lived for two years. Man and wife, ill for several weeks, lay in pitiful surroundings. The patients were on ragged beds, made by themselves. The walls behind the beds were covered with old linen to shut out the wind, which is very cold. There were no windows in the room, but light came through cracks in the walls and the roof. We left the door open so the doctor could see the tongues of his patients. At the fireplace, made with wood covered with clay, sat an old man, worn out by work and grief, delousing a small child. Opposite him was a young woman, the picture of indifference and aloofness, who said, on being questioned by the doctor if she had given the prescribed quantities of quinine to the patients, "Oh, I had forgot it altogether!" Not far from the door, where Turkish wheat and castor beans were growing, stood six to eight short, hollow tree trunks, which served as bee hives. What a contrast! The bees were buzzing and dancing around their simple home, while in the other structure human beings lay in suffering and misery. Had they been better off financially when their farm was started, these people would now be doing well because of their knowledge of the soil. Their indifference to personal comfort is hard to understand. Many families arrive from their former homes to start anew in poor circumstances.

This morning, while riding over the prairies, everything at a distance looked so colorful and attractive. But when you get a closer look, the picture is not so pretty. While passing through a wood, we saw an old tree that had been struck by lightning several years ago. Its shattered trunk and branches were scattered over the ground, offering an interesting subject for an artist to paint.

September 21. For several days it has been raining. The wind, coming from the northwest, is very cold. How dull and monotonous life is when one cannot go outside. Only one miserable tavern in this spot consisting of three houses and a few cabins. No pleasure or entertainment of any kind. Yet the people of the West are not without their pleasures or sprees, as they call them; but what cultivated European wants any part of this atmosphere? These sprees take place at elections, general musters, court days, and the Fourth of July. Brandy and whiskey have to do their best. They start drinking until they are completely intoxicated. Then their pleasure is at its highest point. For instance, the semiannual court took place here. Judge, litigants, jury, and the people were gathered in the courthouse. After the gentlemen of the jury had been addressed pro and con, and the witnesses had been called through the window by the sheriff when their testimony was given, and when all disputes had been settled to the satisfaction of those concerned, everybody went to the tavern where, toward evening, the scene was such as could be described only by the paint brush of a Hogarth. The principal characters in this charming social scene are: the justice of the peace, who is a shoemaker by trade; a Scotsman known as "Doctor"; a captain who fought against Black Hawk in 1832 and who constantly referred to his military exploits; a schoolmaster who was never sober and who was described by the captain as one of his "faithful boys"; the local doctor who, with great dignity, testified in court as a medical authority; several well-dressed county lawyers who discussed the advantages of

America over the rest of the world; a major, a giant of a fellow, who is here to discuss testimony against military men who failed to show up at the last muster. The remaining people were peasants, craftsmen, and other poor-looking souls who got very little attention. After all the heads had been heated, they started singing, screaming, whistling, arguing, and finally fighting. I left the room and went home, but it was impossible to get any rest because the noise continued far into the night.

September 27. Traveled with Doctor Spring at 9 o'clock in the morning to the Little Wabash River, ten miles from Albion. We took a southwest direction, crossed the Boltenhouse Prairie, then [passed] through a thick oak forest. The Little Wabash is just like all other American rivers—wild, dark, and lined with heavy forests. Here and there one encounters a creek, whose water empties into the river. The settlements are poor, populated by Kentuckians who came here about a year ago and are living in company with the wolves. These people do not settle just anywhere. No! They must have a greater range for the hogs and plenty of wild game. These are the main reasons for the migration of the descendants of the famous Kentuckian Daniel Boone. They prefer the wild jungles adjacent to the rivers, because here the herds of deer come to drink. Also, there are areas where the soil contains salt, which attracts the animals. They lick the salt from the soil. These spots are known as "licks." The advantages of the forests and the rivers are offset by the unhealthy vapors that rise from the ground and cause

---

many diseases, in the western states, particularly the ague. We visited nine different log cabins, all unfinished, standing in the midst of the forest and fields of Indian corn. In one of these living quarters I saw a family of twelve living in a single room with four bedsteads. Two patients were in one of the beds. The people looked horrible, especially the children, on whom dirt and filth was like a crust.

These people appear less civilized than the American Indians. Isolated from society, they must of necessity speak a language of their own. When the doctor asked one woman how her mother was, she replied: "Oh, doctor, she is in a mighty wrack of misery." Another woman had "a heap of pain." Someone they don't know is addressed as "Stranger." An old, broken straw chair is pushed toward you with the command, "Stranger, sit down!" And you must sit down. A person in city clothes is referred to as "man." If I had been dressed in rags, I would have been called a gentleman. In front of the door to one of these cabins, someone was butchering a deer and several skins were drying. One deerskin sells for 37 1/2 cents here. On the ground were a few recently caught buffalo fish, probably so called because the head is so large in proportion to the body. They are caught in traps, and the meat is very tough. Here I must not forget to mention that game is not abundant everywhere at all times of the year. At times it is very scarce, and one must be satisfied with bacon and corn. It is also a mistake to think that hunting is an easy business over here. For the American who, from childhood, has roamed the woods and prairies with a gun over his shoulder, taking practice shots at whatever crosses his path, it is very easy. The European immigrant may hunt for weeks without seeing any game. For example, I want to tell one story of the American backwoodsman who had invited me for lunch. He excused the delay in serving the meal, saying, "I expect my boy to shoot some meat first." But the boy was unlucky this time, and the whole family, including their guest, had to eat fried Turkish wheat.

      Evening of October 8. I had in mind to depart from here tomorrow morning, and, according to European custom, I wanted to say goodbye to all my English friends, but a very disgusting scene occurred and I was forced to take part in it. The same day, two Americans had a horrible fight: a colonel of the militia, who was drunk, and another man slightly more sober, who suffered a facial injury. The affair took place in the tavern and was witnessed by the justice of the peace, the sheriff, and another public officer. These three arrested the colonel for disturbing the peace and took him to the courthouse (the workshop of the justice of the peace who was also the local shoemaker). There they wanted to make a record of the incident. It so happened that, as I passed the courthouse, the justice, himself three-quarters drunk, called to me through the window. He said, "Mr. Gustorf, I appoint you to guard this prisoner." At first I thought it was a joke, but then I realized that I was facing a crowd of drunken ruffians who meant business. The justice addressed me again, saying, "I am in earnest, and according to our law have a right to appoint you a guard of the prisoner before the bar, & make you answerable for his not running away." I replied: "I have to travel tomorrow morning and have many things to do. Please choose someone else as watchman." But no, he did not want to do that. The justice appeared to have held a grudge against me because he recently invited me to have a drink in the tavern and I didn't accept his invitation. Willy-nilly, I had to give in, and I approached my prisoner, who sat on a bench with a big knife in his hand. He said to me: "If you come too near, I will run this knife into your guts." His victim lay on the floor, moaning and vomiting. The justice picked up the law book, but either was unable to read or couldn't understand what it said. Another man explained the case to him. Then it was discovered that a sixth juryman was needed, so I was appointed. I was detained until ten o'clock in the evening, when the guilty one, so drunk he couldn't defend himself, was fined five dollars and court costs.

Trip from Albion over the Grand Prairie to Vandalia

October 9. I started this trip at eight o'clock in the morning. My travel companion [was] an American inspector of the National Road, seven miles from Vandalia. Our wagon, a light dearborn, was the best of the shabby vehicles available. Everything went fine until 11 o'clock in the morning, even though the road was bad, but as we approached the Little Wabash we came to a declivity at least 30 feet above the river. There was no bridge or other means of crossing the river. I was shocked because my companion wanted to drive down the steep slope without getting out of the vehicle. I cautioned him against it, but he said there was no danger. He no more than pronounced these words when the wagon, with the greatest impetus, turned over, and the horses dragged it into the river. I escaped with a slight dislocation of the neck and arm, but the wagon was broken at the front end. With great difficulty we unhitched the horses and dragged them and the wagon out of the water. We couldn't have done it by ourselves, but we had help from the people of McSaunder's old mill. Mr. Waterman, my companion, like all Americans who never give up the ship, soon had the necessary tools and materials for repair of the wagon so we could continue our trip. The road got worse. No one in Europe can imagine the condition of these roads. In the prairies the roads are full of deep holes, and there are sloughs in which the horses sink up to their necks. In the woods are the creeks and poorly defined roads where one runs into stumps, which must be moved out of the way of the carriage. If one doesn't want to be in constant fear of breaking a leg or his neck, he should travel through this country on foot. Nevertheless, everybody travels by horse, including emigrants in their big covered wagons, with wife and children, bag and baggage, heading west.

Only Europeans of the peasant class could stand all the hardships of this life. Until seven or eight miles this side of Maysville [now part of Clay City], everything went pretty well, and if Mr. Waterman had followed my advice to drive more slowly, we would have been all right—but no! Hardheaded like all Western Americans, he drove over stick and stone when, all of a sudden, toward sunset, the wagon collapsed again, and we had to leave wagon and baggage at the entrance to the Grand Prairie. Now Waterman took his wife and child on the back of his horse, and I, who cannot ride without a saddle, led the other horse, and so we went about three miles to the next log cabin, where we spent the night. The hut that was supposed to be mine was uncompleted, and the cracks between the logs had not been filled with clay. The roof was open in many places. From where I lay on the floor I could see the cold moon. I couldn't stand the cold and dampness, so I went outside, gathered wood, and made a fire in the stove. I settled down on a broken chair. It was a night without a light, a table, or any books to read. It was unbearable, and each hour was an eternity. Finally the dawn came, and we returned to the wagon. We did a better job than the first time. The morning was cold and damp. When the work was completed after four hours, we breakfasted at the backwoods cabin and then resumed our journey, not at a speedy gallop this time, but very slowly. In Maysville we had a good dinner at Ridgeway['s]. We ate Welsh hens and prairie hens. Venison of the best kind can be bought here for one cent per pound.

Maysville is a small town of five or six log cabins, a tavern, and a little white-and-green shed where Doctor Green has his shop. A sensation here was a long train of emigrants from Kentucky who, with their big wagons filled with slaves, were en route to Missouri. Wives and children were traveling by wagon and on horseback. Toward evening we met them again on the edge of a forest. A big white tent had been erected, at the side of which stood 20 wagons, the horses unhitched. Nearby were big fires, surrounded by men, women, and children, most of them Negroes. This scene in the dark forest, on the edge of a prairie that is three to four hundred miles long and thirty to forty miles wide, was very impressive, combined with a distant prairie fire. These prairie fires can be seen at a distance of sixty miles. During the day, the smoke hangs on the horizon for miles, and at night they look like the lights in a theater. Sometimes these prairie fires are 80 to 100 miles in width, driven by the wind. One fire turned toward us, but luckily it turned again at a distance of about three miles. The screaming of thousands of prairie chickens, partridges, and blackbirds, and their sudden take-off as a traveler approaches, is the only sound in this endless wilderness. To the northwest, the prairie extends to the Kankakee River, not far from Lake Michigan. No mountains, no hills—nothing but wavy grass, with here and there a solitary cabin with its fence. Sometimes the only way to escape from a prairie fire is to unhitch the horses and ride them through a gap in the flames. Settlers on the prairies protect themselves by cutting the grass or by starting backfires in the path of the flames.

Sunday, October 11. Toward noon we arrived at Griffith['s] on the National Road, six miles from Vandalia, with a broken wagon and a lame horse. Here we spent the night.

October 12. Not far from Griffith['s], one enters the forest, which extends on both sides of the National Road to the banks of the Kaskaskia and the high bluff on which is built Vandalia, now the capital of Illinois. The town, which has a population of 800, according to Peck's *Gazetteer*, has not changed since it was founded 15 years ago. If the legislative seat of government were to be moved farther to the north, as planned, the town would disintegrate. The houses, about 100 in all, stand on a very broken soil, and since most of them are log cabins, the whole scene is dark and depressing. One can see about five or six big frame buildings containing stores. The State House is a common brick building. A solitary bank, a wooden church with a small tower, and two or three state offices complete the community of Vandalia. The river is shallow and not navigable. The only facility near the river is an old sawmill, and the river is spanned by two log bridges. Both sides of the river are swampy to the edge of the forest, making the climate very unhealthy in the summertime. One can see signs of ague and other diseases on the faces of the people. The city has little or no trade, and the stores get their supplies from St. Louis. The surrounding farms are poor because the soil is not fertile, and therefore Congress land is available. The best soil is on the Wakefield Prairie, which is very flat and surrounded by thick forests.

There are five or six Germans here, craftsmen, grocers, and whiskey buyers, all that remain of 81 Germans brought here from Hannover by Herr Ernst to found a colony, but like many others in such enterprises, he lost his life and $40,000.[11] I visited his widow who, with her daughter, is still in mourning. A few days ago a young German from Hannover killed himself with a double-barreled gun. Desperation brought him to this end. I watched the building of the National Road, a gigantic task. Because of a shortage of labor and money, the work is proceeding very slowly. At times only four laborers worked on a stretch of one mile where at least 40 should be employed. One section outside Vandalia cost 70,000 dollars. Since Jefferson's Presidency, the work has been carried on with very little accomplished. "Wanted: 700 workmen on the Cumberland Road." This notice has been printed in the newspaper all summer long. A few Polish officers worked on this job for 70 cents per day.[12]

October 13. The Vandalia Inn where I spent the night was airtight and the bed was free of bugs. I paid one dollar for room and three meals. The town's aristocratic people (each Western town has such) were: employees of the National Road who wore eagles on their threadbare clothes; two or three officials; a few lawyers; and a big judge named [John York] Sawyer. This individual is a funny, fat fellow. On my arrival yesterday, when I asked about him, I was informed that he is the biggest man in town. Why, is he really so great? I asked. "Yes, sir, he weighs three hundred pounds." In the beginning I was astonished at his size and importance because Americans check their weight, and I was really impressed with his size when I saw him in the company of other guests at the tavern. At eight o'clock in

---

11 In 1819, Ferdinand Ernst, a native of the Kingdom of Hannover and a gentleman of wealth and literary taste, according to Randall Parrish, in *Historic Illinois* (Chicago, 1905), 347, had brought to Vandalia, newly selected site of the state capital, a colony of about thirty German families. The *Journal of the Illinois State Historical Society*, XXXIV (October, 1931), 404, gives the date as 1820 and states that Ernst paid all the expenses of the move. His "Travels in Illinois in 1819" was published in the Society's *Transactions* for the year 1903, pp. 150–65.

12 The influence of the Cumberland or National Road (part of the present-day U. S. 40) upon the development of the Ohio and upper Mississippi valleys

the morning, I traveled by United States Mail to St. Louis. The
day was fair and warm, like Europe in June, and I was very
happy to have no traveling companions. My driver was a nice
young fellow, very unusual in this country where roughness and
brutality are common characteristics. At 11 o'clock we stopped
at the Post Office in Mulberry Grove, a name which in Germany
would suggest an earthly Paradise, but I could find no similarity;
but that's the way it is in this country—everything has grand
appellations but in reality is nothing but wretchedness.

In the woods here I noticed the odd way they mark the roads
and the county lines. Three notches cut in the trunk of a tree
indicate the main road. To mark a county boundary, a section of
bark is removed and the beginning letters of the county name
are carved in the wood beneath. This is an amusing way to travel
these untrod roads.

Soon afterwards I arrived in Greenville on the Fork Prairie.
The town already is deteriorating. As many small towns in this
country see the light of day, others disappear. Since the National Road will bypass this little town, the inhabitants fear that
it will be doomed. Toward four o'clock at the Post Office at the
entrance to Looking Glass Prairie, probably so called because
it is as smooth, polished, and even as a mirror. One can travel
for miles and the forest on the far horizon looks like the shore
line from the open sea. Here and there stand solitary and lonesome farms in the open prairie without a single tree to provide
shade. Now and then one sees a log house built against the side
of a small, round hill for protection against wind and weather.

---

was considerable. Work began in 1811 at Cumberland, Maryland, the eastern
terminus, and by 1818 the United States mail was transported over it to
Wheeling, Virginia, the route generally following what had been known as
Braddock's Road. In March, 1825, Congress appropriated funds for a turnpike
to Zanesville, Ohio, along Zane's Trace, and later voted additional funds for
its extension through Indiana and Illinois. It was completed to Vandalia,
Illinois, after the Federal Government relinquished control. The 591 miles
from Cumberland to Vandalia cost about $7 million in federal funds. The last
congressional appropriation was made in 1838, but a small amount was voted
in 1844 for a survey between Vandalia and Jefferson City, Missouri.

Next is the Ridge Prairie, probably named for the frequent ridges. The constant chirping of crickets in the grass is heard all day and even more at night. From the nearby woods comes a penetrating, disagreeable smell of decaying vegetation, which is a hazard to the health of human beings.

In the evening I sought shelter from Mr. Street, a Yankee in the Marine Settlement. Here I asked about New Switzerland which was founded by Dr. Köpfli.[13] My host pointed out a nearby German from Hamburg, who was not a member of the company, but who gave me a saddening description of his own predicament and that of others. Since May he has worked on Ripley's farm. He, himself, his wife and children were stricken by fever and no one gave them a helping hand because maid-servants are not available here. He was so sick that he tried to sell the farm, but even at the low price of 400 dollars there were no buyers.

At Edwardsville, on the edge of Ridge Prairie, a small town with colorfully painted frame houses and stores in abundance, we had breakfast in the stage house. The proprietor, whom I took for an Englishman because of his polite manners, told me he was from Charleston, South Carolina. He bought this stage house a few years ago. Like all planters in South Carolina, he was very dignified and obliging. Gerke and son lived for quite some time in his house.[14] The latter is married to an American woman who provided him with a sizable fortune, and therefore he is very well off. Also, he has received an inheritance from his wife's relatives. When we drove by a vegetable garden, my

13 In We Who Built America (New York, 1940), 301, Dr. Karl Wittke identified Dr. Kaspar Köpfli as one of the founders of a Swiss immigrant colony at Highland, Illinois, originally known as Helvetia. Some of its members found employment as farm hands and others in the local brewery.

14 Dr. Henry C. Gerke and son William emigrated to Madison County in 1824 and brought the remainder of the family from Cassel ten years later. Gerke's books on conditions in the Mississippi Valley, published in Hamburg, were widely read in Germany. William, the elder of his two sons, settled in Marine Township in 1831. John, an artist, came to the United States with his mother in 1834 and died in St. Louis in 1847.

driver, who was not the same one as yesterday, said, "I have a notion of having some turnips." So saying, he climbed over the fence and cut a good portion with his knife with not the slightest feeling of guilt. He also picked pawpaws in the woods that, he said, belonged to Uncle Sam, and as a citizen he had a right to do so. He was brave enough to offer me a few. It is an oval, yellow-green fruit, juicy and well-tasting, the inside being very similar to the color of apricots. The seeds are like big black beans. This edible fruit grows wild in the woods.

Here in the West, one frequently sees the great Washington on tavern signs. In the evening we stopped at Washington Hall. My driver gentleman said, "I have to seek shelter here and should, like western folks do, have a glass of brandy." He was surprised to hear me inquire about hotel prices in St. Louis, and because I didn't care for a glass of brandy, my driver thought I wasn't much of a gentleman. The hall of that great hero of olden times was an old, weather-beaten frame house with broken windows, on the edge of a small but abundant prairie.

Nine miles from St. Louis we passed on the right a muddy lake and on the left a chain of small hills, the first I have seen in this state.[15] Already one notices the nearness of the great river. We are on the so-called American Bottom. It is a plain of black soil with a few bald hills. One sees many poor huts, surrounded by corn fields. After a while one reaches Illinoistown [East St. Louis], an insignificant spot on the Cahokia River, crossed by a wooden bridge. The sight of the Mississippi, father of all rivers, which is one mile wide at this point, is a great surprise after my

---

[15] Travelers and settlers in the area did not realize that these small hills form the largest group of Indian burial and domiciliary mounds in the United States. The muddy water on his right was a sluggish stream or slough known as Long Lake, a tributary of the Cahokia River. One of the "few bald hills" rising above the plain was to become known as the Great Cahokia or Monk's Mound. John Francis Snyder, writing in the *Journal of the Illinois State Historical Society*, II (July, 1909), 71–92, described this area as the "richest field of archeological research in the state of Illinois, if not in the entire United States." The small, round hills on Looking Glass Prairie that, as Gustorf noted, provided occasional log cabins with shelter against the weather, also were burial mounds.

long stay in Albion. Standing on the east bank of this huge river and looking across at the fresh and youthful city of the Holy Louis, with its towers, white houses, and large steamboats, is a pleasure to the eye and an inspiration to the mind.

We drove down to the steam ferry.

October 15. I spent the night at the National Hotel. Customs and inconveniences are the same here as everywhere in the eastern states; as expensive, often even more so; but a bad guesthouse is a palace in comparison with the dirty and poorly built log cabins where wind and weather come through the walls. After all those sleepless nights on a hard floor, a bed here is better than a divan. About noon I moved into a boarding-house near the Mississippi and owned by a German named Atorf. In this house, as in others, I met many people who came here from all parts of Germany, enticed to this country by the propaganda of Duden and Gerke. Many of them bought farms when they first arrived and have since sold or rented them if they had an opportunity to do so, because they lost their money and their health trying to make a success of farming. Their stories of hardship and suffering are all the same and are too numerous to describe here. The livestock died, the grain rotted on the stalk. One man was cheated by his hired help; another lost his wife and children. A third man was deserted by his la-borers at harvest time after he had paid them a dollar and a half a day and treated them well.*

---

* Journal continues, page 74.

During these first eleven days in the city the visitor precipitated himself wholeheartedly into the Duden controversy and allowed himself to be convinced by the many disaffected German farmers and ex-farmers with whom he talked that the once popular writer had deliberately misrepresented conditions on the American frontier in his unsuccessful efforts to establish a German colony in Missouri. As a matter of fact, Dr. Gottfried Duden, who had established a colony for German immigrants about four miles north of Washington, Missouri, in 1824, wrote many enthusiastic letters to friends in Germany, extolling the fertility of the soil and the advantages of frontier living. But he warned specifically of the disadvantages and dangers of the frontier for those persons who were not accustomed to hard work and had no money to pay for experienced help. These letters, published in Germany at the writer's expense in 1829 by Sam Lucas of Elberfeld under the title *Bericht über eine Reise nach den westlichen Staaten Nordamerikas*, stimulated considerable emigration of Germans into the backwoods near St. Louis. The book was reprinted at St. Gallen, Switzerland, in 1832 and at Bonn in 1834.

Unfortunately, many of the readers of Duden's letters did not heed his advice regarding the importance of making adequate preparations for coping with the hardships of backwoods living. None of Duden's letters mentions why he rented his own farm to a tenant and returned to Germany in 1827, nor does he appear to have been aware of any feeling of resentment toward him by his German neighbors, as recorded by Gustorf in his journal nine years later. Since Duden and his book are mentioned so often in the Journal, most of the references being unfavorable, an examination of the collected letters is essential to an understanding of his motives and for the purpose of determining why he was so bitterly denounced by the German immigrants of St. Louis and vicinity. The following extracts from his thirty-first letter, written in March of 1827, absolve Doctor Duden of all accusations more serious than the possession of abundant enthusiasm, confidence, and faith in the future of the upper Mississippi Valley:

> How often have I thought of the poor German people. How
> much more abundance of everything there is in this country
> and how much more the German farmers would accomplish

with this fertile soil. There is room on the Missouri for a million more beautiful plantations, not to mention the other rivers.

The great fertility of the soil, the extent of which is tremendous, the mild climate, the ideal river connections, the freedom of movement throughout several thousand miles, the complete security of individuals and their possessions, low taxes—all these are the things which put Americans ahead of people in other countries. In what country on this Earth do you find all these advantages? In order to describe this situation further, I have only to remind you of the richness of the forests, the abundance of coal, salt, iron, lead, copper, saltpeter, and other minerals, as well as the booming steamship business; and finally, in contrast to the European prejudices with respect to the ranks of trade and physical labor, only those people who have been farmers in Europe, especially Germany, can appreciate the significance of the seven products I have mentioned. Any farmer will know what it means to have to pay no attention to the livestock; when neither horsebreeding nor the fattening of cattle and hogs depend upon the cultivation of the soil. On the whole, it is sufficient to buy only a stem pair and leave the rest to nature. He can judge the value of the soil when, year after year, without fertilization, it produces good crops. In Germany, if the soil is not cultivated, it produces very little.

Nevertheless, I would not advise anyone to come here without making the proper preparations, and I would not advise anyone to come alone. Whoever survives the first two years is on the safe side, for they are the most difficult because of the change in climate, the hardships of domestic life, and homesickness, all of which can affect the healthiest body and endanger the lives of the people. These are the hazards which have been confronted by many colonists who emigrated to distant lands. These changes in living conditions cause many people to fail and have no connection with the country itself. To the children of immigrants born in the new country, these hardships are of little concern. I am convinced that when twenty or thirty German families live here under comfortable circumstances, they will have no desire to return to Europe. They will want to see it again, but will have no desire to live there.

In the light of the foregoing statement that German immigrants would want to see Europe again but would have no desire to live there, it is interesting to note that Duden himself, after living only three years in the colony, returned to Europe and remained there. While thousands of Germans, inspired by his published and widely read letters, were emigrating to the western frontier, Duden indicated that he was contemplating a second trip to America in 1837. There is no record, however, that he undertook a second journey. It is reasonable to assume, therefore, that word of the ill feelings against him among the German immigrants in St. Louis and vicinity, as noted by Gustorf and other objective observers, caused Duden to abandon or postpone indefinitely his plans to return to the colony.

Extracts from Duden's thirty-first letter conclude with the following detailed explanation of costs in terms of the thaler, which then was the equivalent of seventy-four cents:

German immigrants are very welcome here. As soon as they have entered the country they have the same privileges as citizens except the right to vote, which is granted after five years' residence. I have mentioned previously that in the state of Missouri an alien can buy his own land. . . . The purchase of land in connection with the development of towns is a secure investment. The land west of the Mississippi is terra incognita to the scientists. Investigation of land values and uses would cost very little. . . . How many men in Germany possess between four and six thousand thaler with no other prospect than to live on it? Yet this is more than enough for the lucky family that lives on the banks of the Missouri; however, one must deduct 800 to 1,000 thaler for travel expenses (400 thaler equal 540 Dutch gulden). With this sum the immigrant can buy two adult horses, male and female, which cost about 120 thaler; furthermore, he can afford to raise a large family and live comfortably at a cost that in

Germany would be six times as much. A person who is able to cultivate his own soil would need no more than 1,000 thaler plus the cost of transportation. I estimate 150 to 200 thaler for 80 acres of land; 45 to 60 thaler for clearing and fencing five to seven acres; 120 thaler for two horses; 26 thaler for two cows; 12 thaler for two sows; 100 thaler for buildings and the same amount for furniture and equipment. All together, 618 thaler, with almost 400 thaler remaining for less important expenses. If one spends an additional 200 thaler for housing, the immigrant is much better off than peasants who till their own land in Germany. A quarter of a mile from here lives a planter named Jacob Haun. He started his establishment seven years ago. Since he had barely 100 thaler in the beginning, Haun lived and worked on Government land and earned enough money to buy 160 acres; then he worked his own land without help. Everything went fine and in seven years he accumulated 3,000 thaler. Meanwhile, his wife has borne him five children. His household consumes annually more than 1,200 pounds of pork, one ox between five and six hundred pounds, and several dozen chickens. Furthermore, he killed about ten or twelve deer and many turkeys. Who would believe that a household of two adults and five children under six years of age require so much meat? Of course, you must take into account the hospitality extended to visitors.

The foregoing statements apply only to those immigrants who are willing to become farmers and cultivate their own soil. The opportunities for farming as I have described them are so bright that even if millions of immigrants arrive in this century, the circumstances will remain unchanged. . . . There are a few occupations that do not prosper here, but in addition to farming there is a demand for tanners, skilled mechanics, joiners, cabinet-makers, bricklayers, carpenters, saddlers, and blacksmiths. The tanners will find that skins and tanning materials are plentiful; nevertheless, leather is expensive. Saddlers must remember that nobody here travels on foot. Glass factories are rare. A common bottle in St. Louis costs 12½ cents. The same situation applies to pottery. Brewers would become rich very fast on the Mississippi, but they would have to supervise the cultivation of grain and hops, which so far has been neglected. St. Louis imports beer from Pittsburgh and the Atlantic Coast. Anyone with a knowledge of pharmaceuticals will find a great future in the western states. I need not mention that builders are in great demand because of the rapidity with which towns are springing up. Craftsmen should settle in or near the cities where medical care is available. Under no circumstances should anyone emigrate without money.

It is assumed that Gustorf was among the thousands of Germans who had read Duden's letters and had been influenced by the writer to investigate the immigrant colonies in the vicinity of St. Louis and possibly to invest a part of his capital in land or some type of private enterprise such as a grocery, tavern, or boardinghouse. This assumption would explain his apprenticeship in farming in Albion and his obvious interest in private enterprises of the kinds he described. Ironically, at the time of his death in Peoria, Illinois, he had just returned from New Orleans with merchandise for a retail store that he intended to open there.

[October 15 resumes.] *Wherever I go, Duden and Gerke are maligned, and I have been told how the people who settled near Duden's farm destroyed the property because of sheer exasperation. Many people who were able to recover some cash from the sale of their farms, fed up with farming and farm life, have gone back to Europe, cured of all extravagant ideas of American freedom, culture, and fellowship in the West. The only people who can better themselves in this country are the common classes, day laborers, and craftsmen. Despite their complaints about the climate, they can earn a living with their hands, and as time passes they accumulate enough money to buy a piece of property. They are satisfied as long as they have enough to eat.*

More than 300 German people died in this town last year. Entire families died within a few days. I see many people who still bear the signs of illness on their faces.

This afternoon I wandered through the entire town. The population is 12,000, and the only difference between this and other American towns of the same size is the great number of log houses built by the first settlers, who were Frenchmen. These first houses are poorly built, but with emphasis on style. These original houses are giving way gradually to the stone and brick dwellings being built by Americans coming from the East. One sees a few large limestone buildings, especially on Water Street, which runs parallel to the river. They are mostly warehouses. The streets are parallel to the river, crossed by other streets. Main Street is the principal business district. Other streets are not completed because building is in progress everywhere.

In the southwestern part of town, where the streets end, are many poor houses where descendants of the first French settlers live. Although they appear very poor and sickly, they are supposed to possess considerable wealth because they are the original owners of the land on which the town is being built. Like all Frenchmen abroad, they cling to their traditions and primitive way of life and even today can speak little or no English. Public buildings here consist of a few churches and the City Hall. Of the former, the Catholic cathedral[16] merits attention. It is built in good taste—not American—of limestone, which is found on the west bank of the Mississippi in great quantity. A beautiful and massive colonnade adorns the entrance, on either side of which is found the following inscription:

DEO UNI ET TRINO

In Honorem S Ludovici   Dictatum A D MDCCCXXXIV.
my house shall be called   ma maison sera appellée
the house of prayer.   la maison de prière.

It is curious how the Catholics in the western states fight for their beliefs and the other sects try to interest the people. They are constantly fighting each other, but so far only with the pen. The Reverend Doctor Beecher of Cincinnati believes that public revolution through the power of the Catholic Church is imminent. Of course it is true that they have the most beautiful churches as well as a few well-built colleges and other institutions. That all this strife is caused by European influence to

---

16 The Catholic cathedral, now known as the Old Cathedral, is the only historic building described here by the traveler that remains on the St. Louis water front. Restored in good taste, it still merits attention, but unfortunately the site is dominated by the Jefferson National Expansion Memorial, erected to commemorate the 200th anniversary of the city that was founded by French trappers in 1767.

bring about a political revolution is difficult to believe. Only spiritual arrogance can entertain such thoughts.

Another building that pleased me very much is the new market on Market Street, located near the water front. Out front is the meat market, where the meat is cut on huge log blocks reminiscent of the American wilderness. On top of the building is a small tower with a very decorative clock. In front of the building is a small, open square where the farmers stand with their wagons, which are not pulled by beautiful strong horses, as in Philadelphia, but by oxen.

Today I also visited the world-famous "Storehouse of the American Fur Company," where great quantities of furs of all kinds can be seen. Indians and Negroes were busy folding the furs. The Indians are brought here by the trappers and hunters from their excursions to the Rocky Mountains, probably because they are so skilled in the treatment of the furs, particularly the buffalo.

October 16. The food in my boardinghouse is good, but everything else is unsatisfactory. The most unpleasant thing is the bedbugs that make sleeping impossible. They are all over town and are practically impossible to exterminate. I put my straw sack on the floor, but I was made almost ill by these malicious vampires. A terrific storm raged all night and it was bitterly cold. Near dawn there was a strong downpour that continued all day, forcing me to stay at home. During the day I met many cultured Germans, former farmers, now earning their bread and butter in a very humble way. One German gentleman from the vicinity of Hannover told me several sad stories about the suffering and hardship of several middle-class German families in Missouri and Illinois. Their experiences are beyond imagination. With their wives, sons, and daughters they live wretched lives. Imagine people from the finest German classes living in miserable huts! Previously they had lived in comfortable houses, and now they have to eat the plainest of food and do the hardest work in the fields, surrounded by black forests and cut off from society and all the conveniences of life. They live in memory of the sweet past, in contrast with the miserable present, and in contemplation of a sad future, one illusion after another. It is not always easy to give the appearance of contentment when one's heart and mind are suffering from regret. Their despair can be read in the deep, dark lines in their faces.

October 18. Beautiful weather! Yesterday I roamed through several sections of the town. The center still looks very depressing. There are still too many log cabins and poor huts, all occupied. There is a great demand for more houses and apartments, and many Eastern merchants who wanted to do business in the city, couldn't find suitable living quarters, so they canceled their plans. They are building everywhere, but still not enough to satisfy the demand. The main reason for the shortage of houses is the high cost of land. Landowners are mostly Frenchmen. Descendants of the first settlers have made fortunes from the sale of land. For example: the Chouteaus [Auguste and Pierre], whose house on Main Street is built in the old Spanish style, own lots that are valued at 160,000 dollars. But they refuse to sell and do not build on the lots themselves, hoping that the value will increase. Their house, built many years ago, is still protected by the wall that was used in defense against the attacks of hostile Indians.

Educational institutions like those in the East do not exist here. If one wants to read the news, he must go into a tavern where mostly Western papers are available. Nobody is interested in magazines or literary reviews. All they are interested in is local gossip and political activities.

Last night I went to the German club. It is very new and there are not many members. In the reading room there were supposed to be newspapers in all languages, but I found only one, the St. Louis Republican. While reading matter was scarce, I saw plenty of whiskey, beer, and grog. The members are all cultured German people, lukewarm republicans who, despite their republicanism, cling to their former titles such as "Herr Oberst, Herr Hauptman" et cetera. But all this wouldn't be so bad, since the Americans have their colonels, captains, and squires, but Herr Graf! Imagine a German count leaving his own country because of his republican sympathies! Most of them should be returned to Europe and the monarchist environment they left behind instead of remaining here as humiliated republicans. The place where this group meets is owned by a Pole named Clopicki.[17] This man of distinguished

---

[17] Gustave Koerner, Memoirs of Gustave Koerner, 1809–1896, Thomas J. McCormack, ed. (Torch Press, Cedar Rapids, 1909), I, 332–33: "I must mention a very comical visitor, Major Clopike [sic], a Pole. There had arrived in 1833 several hundred Poles, who, entering Austrian territory, after the fall of Warsaw, and being disarmed and kept there under surveillance, had finally been shipped by the Austrian government (I believe in a vessel of the American Navy) to the United States. Congress had donated to them several thousand acres of public land, not yet sold, in some of the Western States. The Poles had appointed a committee to inspect these lands. . . . Clopike was one of these commissioners and had now become a resident of St. Louis where he had established a coffee-house. He was a very tall, imposing-looking man of more

appearance and excellent manner owns a tavern in an isolated street.

Yesterday, from Mr. Christian Bimpage, who publishes a German newspaper, I received a pamphlet against Duden, written by Gustav Körner in Belleville and printed in Frankfurt am Main.[18] This article is too general in nature. The author should have been more specific. It is obvious that Körner withholds many facts that, for reasons of his own, are not revealed in his pamphlet. He should speak freely, if his real purpose is to be of help to his countrymen, and bring out everything against Duden that from personal experience and observation he knows to be the truth. Only the German poet Heine has truthfully described the hardship and suffering of the cultured German immigrants who settled in the western states of America.

I have just returned from a visit to the Catholic church. The interior is quite nice and simply decorated except for the frescoes at the windows. They depict scenes from the life of Christ, with English titles. I also saw an oil painting entitled "Donné par le Roi de France 1818." The choir impressed me very much. Since one hears so much miserable bawling in the churches of America, where there is little appreciation of the finer arts, this choir was a pleasant surprise. Members of the choir were from the Sisters of Mercy, led by a German tenor. Their singing was very gracious, and it touched my heart. The organist was tolerable. I believe that the Catholics in this country care more for good music than the other denomina-

---

than fifty years of age, of rather handsome and martial features, spoke French fluently and German passably."

18 Koerner, in his "Review of Duden's Report Concerning the Western States of America," 326, written in 1834 when he was known as Gustav Philipp Körner, stated: "I agree with Duden that emigration may become a necessity, and, if properly conducted, is of advantage to the emigrant. I do not essentially differ in my views of the subject from him; nevertheless, I cannot subscribe to many of them, and I deem his 'Report' of the region of the country of which he speaks and of the conditions the emigrants are expected to find there, as too flattering and too vividly colored."

tions, whose singing and organ music is intolerable. The sermon was delivered in the French language. After the service, I inspected the feminine sex, who are always to be seen in the American churches. Most of them were of French descent, as revealed by their poise and style of clothing. Others are of mixed blood, including Indian. They are of small build, with yellow complexion. The younger women have grace and charm in their features, but they are few in number. One sees Anglo-Americans, Creoles, Spaniards, Germans, and French. The Germans and Swiss are easily identified either by the cut of their clothes or by their hats. By printed signs on the wall, visitors were enjoined not to spit on the floor, to remove their hats during the service, and not to damage the walls.

This afternoon, despite cold and unfriendly weather, I walked a few miles upriver and away from the town. Everything looks very desolate and dreary; old frame houses and ploughed fields; seldom does one see a house that could be termed comfortable and beautiful to look at. I climbed a conical hill that had been used by the Indians as a burying ground. It is called the "Big Mound." I imagine there are plenty of Indian skulls underneath the ground here. The view from the hill includes flat ground covered with forest and the dull, milky waters of the Mississippi creeping seaward.

It started to rain very hard, and I sought shelter in the first house, which belonged to a peasant from Baden, Germany, who was still dressed in his native red broadcloth vest. He rented house and land for five dollars per month. This man seemed to be quite a sensible fellow, because when I asked him why he didn't buy his own land, he told me: "It is better to live in the city where one can make more money, than on a farm where the work is hard and the food is plain." Furthermore, he said, he prefers to leave the farming to the more distinguished Germans. What a reversed situation here! The German farmers became townspeople and vice versa; the first ones are called "gentlemen" and enjoy everything in abundance, and the latter are starving on the so-called fertile soil, taking refuge in the whiskey bottle and trying to give an impression of gaiety, but their unhappiness is written on their faces. For example, there is Mr. von Bock who wants to go back to Germany. "What does he do?" I asked my host. "Does he own a grocery?" "A grossery, no," he replied, "rather a kleinery!" And I thought to myself, poor Mr. Bock, what kind of buck have you shot?[19] Then I went into the grocery of the neighbor, Bock, and asked for a glass of beer.[20] Mrs. Bock, standing by the door, said she had no beer because her husband was ill with fever. Her small daughter, Emilie, was playing in front of the store, her bright face a contrast to the sad features of the mother.

October 20. Whereas the water of the Ohio is dull, the water of the Mississippi is brown from the mud. It has a purging effect on newcomers to St. Louis, temporarily with some people and permanently with others. In my case it is temporary, although I was sick throughout the night, suffering from

---

[19] Gustorf and his host are exchanging German puns at the expense of Mr. Bock.

[20] In "The Old French Towns of Illinois," *Journal of the Illinois State Historical Society*, XXXVI (December, 1943), 345–67, John Francis Snyder identified the frontier grocery as a dramshop or bar "not yet dignified by the title of saloon." Drygoods, hardware, and conventional nutriment were obtainable in the so-called general store. The frontier tavern, where beer, wine, and whiskey usually were available, also provided meals and lodging. The exact nature of the frontier grocery becomes apparent as the journal progresses.

diarrhea. As in many cities of the East, this water is pumped into a reservoir on a hill. There the water can settle and therefore is not as unclean as that which is taken immediately from the river. This reservoir provides a part of the city with water.

No European can imagine the human hustle and bustle on Main Street and up and down Water Street, where people of all races and colors can be seen: Americans from the eastern states; Frenchmen from New Orleans (or born here); Negroes of all shades; Germans who have lived here for several years and who look quite Americanized; German peasants, newly arrived, who still run around in their native dress; Indians of all the different tribes, at whom the peasants stare in open curiosity and who, because of their awkward behavior, attract everybody's attention.

In the market square the farmers sell their produce from their wagons; others sell horses. These people, especially the backwoodsmen, are very poor looking, a certain indifference being apparent in their whole appearance and demeanor. Coat and trousers are made of a dark reddish stuff called "homespun," shabby and often torn. Their hats are tattered, often without a crown, and with split brim. They wear a kind of half boot, seldom oiled or polished and very shabby from constant wear. These people never own more than one pair of boots; when they purchase a new pair, their old ones are discarded in front of the shoe store. I saw a group of people staring at a Sack [sic] Indian, stoic in posture and clad in a woolen blanket. Another crowd gathered around two men who were fighting with their fists.

"Let them have fair play," several people screamed; others yelled to let them alone. The fighters, encouraged by the crowd, continued until their mouths and noses were streaming with blood. The crowd loved it. Boys as well as men fight this way in the streets, and instead of separating them, the people shout encouragement. Today I saw several German students, doctors, professors, officers, and officials. When one sees these people in their present condition and learns of their origin, the metamorphosis in their natures is unbelievable. A former Heidelberg student, filthy from head to toe, is now a typesetter in a local print shop, prolonging the misery of his life. A former professor, now a farmer, is climbing onto his cart, a jug of whiskey in his hand. A Hessian captain is now a partner with a former official from Baden in a grocery business (the last refuge of the unhappy ones), having lost all his capital in an unsuccessful farming venture. It is amusing to see a German aristocrat, now a tavern owner, who does not understand enough English to distinguish gin from brandy and rum from whiskey to serve his thirsty American patrons.

When a boy asked for soap, the former captain sold him sugar; and when a customer desires to change a ten-dollar bill, he is unable to distinguish between good money and bad. The captain should be sent back to his Hessian guard mount. Another German aristocrat owns a grocery with a private bar catering only to rich Germans (one must not think that class consciousness ceases to exist among the Germans in America). Here I met a Pole, a doctor from Cassel, and several PhD's from

Frankfurt, with their wives. They were drinking Franz wine and talking in their peculiar dialect about "a calf, a pig, and a cow's chain" purchased by one of the doctors at an auction sale. Another gentleman, who was reading a German newspaper from Philadelphia, became very angry about the fuss made in the German-American newspapers against the German princes. I took a student home with me who looked as if he had tuberculosis. On the way he described his various illnesses since landing in Baltimore: gall bladder infection, inflammation of the brain, and smallpox; how he was robbed of his money by other German people; and how hard he had worked on a farm to earn his living. Now he hopes that all his troubles are over because he is expecting permission from his parents to return home to Germany.

Walk to the Prairie House

Wherever I went, to taverns, groceries, and social affairs, I heard about the Prairie House, the pleasure spot of St. Louis. Even the Germans spoke of it as something special. I made up my mind to visit it this afternoon. It is three miles from here. The road is the most uninteresting one I have ever seen—nothing but swamps covered with brush. Then the scenery opens to permit a view of the wooded hills. Before approaching the Prairie House itself, one must cross the race track upon which stood a board fence and a shed, both painted white and probably built for the use of the spectators. Farther on is a brick building with a big sign, "Prairie House." There is no garden or attractive park—just a big tavern with a barroom. Two "gentlemen" were sitting in front of the door, chatting about a "fat pig," while a lady in one of the rooms sang "Robin Adair" to piano accompaniment. Nearby thousands of crows and jackdaws were screaming and a pig was dying a miserable death.

The Horse Bratwurst Machine
of a German Butcher

Because of the eagerness to make money in this country, one encounters all kinds of strange enterprises. Today, when I was walking near the edge of town where the butchers live, I heard a very peculiar rattling noise. I went closer and observed a chopping machine operated by horsepower. Large chunks of meat were being chopped very fine by knives in a large receptacle. Another machine was stuffing the ground meat into animal intestines. It worked so fast that within a few minutes the table was covered with beautiful *bratwurst*. The proprietor of this sausage factory is a German who lives in a very pretty brick house near his factory, which, he said, would shortly be operated by steam rather than by horse power.

October 22. In the lower part of town, near the Mississippi, live the poorer classes in small huts, old Spanish houses, and recently built log cabins. The air is bad and must be very unhealthy. There the Mississippi has formed an island to which leads a muddy, and in summer completely dried-up, river bed that is as wide as the Main at Frankfurt. At high water the island is almost completely inundated, but there are a few small huts on it. For the poorer classes, this island is an advantage because it is loaded with tree trunks that are carried downstream in the spring floods. They provide a convenient source of firewood for the people who live nearby, who chop them up and haul away the wood in wheelbarrows. This driftwood is useful in the winter because other sources are so far away.

Sunday, October 24. Written at St. Charles on the Missouri River.—At ten o'clock in the morning I traveled in company of three Germans from St. Louis to St. Charles. Twenty miles is the distance, and we made the trip in four hours in a rented wagon. The road to the Missouri runs partly over flat land and partly through hills covered by forests. Before reaching the banks of the Missouri, one must cross the so-called bottom land, a black, muddy soil that is completely covered by water at flood stage. The wagon is brought to a halt on a steam ferry that crosses the river. At this time of the year the Missouri is not nearly so wide as the Mississippi, but the current is much stronger. St. Charles is located on a bluff and has one street and a few scattered houses. The town is one of the oldest in the state of Missouri, inhabited by Frenchmen and Germans. From a little hill where the Catholics have built a chapel and a cloister, one gets a nice view of the surrounding country. The banks of the Missouri are thinly populated, the land being mostly a virgin wilderness. In a grocery I met several Germans, all planning to become farmers. One of them was a doctor from Hamburg who was enthusiastic over the life of a farmer, but I got the impression he was not being entirely frank with me because I was a stranger.

These people emptied one glass of whiskey after another. A Swiss who had just returned from Santa Fe joined our group. Another German came in and angrily told us about the way some of the German settlers cheat and rob their fellow Germans. He, himself, had just been robbed of ten dollars. These German people make themselves more miserable by arguing and gossiping. It is a shame to see strong men, who could have been very useful to their own country, wasting their time and talent, abandoning their professional careers, and trying to start a new life in this wilderness. There are exceptions, of course, but they are scarce.

October 25. By accident this morning, I met the same group of Germans. The Hamburg doctor made a spontaneous reference to Duden, saying: "How did he get us into this situation?" Then another German read a Duden description of life on an American farm. Still another related how Duden would postpone certain farming tasks when the weather was hot, saying that he "would do it in the cool season." This phrase became popular, especially among the backwoodsmen. Whenever they didn't feel like doing something, they would say: "We'll do it in the cool season."

"Yes, Duden and Gerke did indeed pull us by the nose, and this nose was a damned long trunk," commented another member of the group. "Better to die in Europe than to live in misery here," he added. A man from Göttingen said: "Better to return to Germany and live with a sword in one hand and human dignity in the other, as recommended by Chateaubriand."[21]

---

[21] René de Chateaubriand (1768–1848), French writer and statesman; author of *The Spirit of Christendom* and *René*.

Serious illness, including an eye ailment, incapacitated Frederick Julius Gustorf on the eleventh day of his visit in St. Louis, which prevented him from making further entries until April 28, 1836. When he resumed writing on that date, he said: "What a long intermission in my diary, caused by suffering. From October 25th, when I wrote last, until a few weeks ago, nothing but suffering, disease, and inconveniences of all kinds; and the most horrible of all is that since last December I have been deprived of the use of my eyes. If I had been able to write or to dictate, then I wouldn't have been so depressed mentally."

While staying with Mr. and Mrs. Flower in Albion, Illinois, Gustorf had met John Benson, a young British immigrant whose family had settled on the prairie near Peoria, Illinois. When the journal was resumed following his long illness in St. Louis, it is not surprising, therefore, to learn that the journalist was recording his experiences as he traveled on board a river steamer to Peoria. A visit to John Benson and his family, Gustorf had decided, would give him a chance to rest and regain his strength while meeting and talking with another group of European immigrants.

The day before the boat reached Peoria, however, his eyes began to trouble him again, and he was unable to make any entries in his journal until he had been with the Bensons on their Limestone Prairie farm for two weeks. His own difficulties, however, seemed unimportant by comparison with the hardships that this English family were confronting. The elder John Benson, a former barrister in Thorne, Yorkshire, had been killed by the accidental discharge of his own double-barreled gun on the threshold of his newly completed prairie home. Harriet Coupland Benson, the mother, died soon thereafter from grief and complications. Harriet, the eldest of the six children, was twenty-two years of age when her brother's German friend arrived for a visit in their impoverished home.

Entries in the journal during the visitor's stay with the family reveal a growing interest in the "extremely charming Englishwoman whose careful education fitted her for life in the best of London society." In the diary, at least, he began referring to her as "my charming Englishwoman." And what were Harriet's impressions of her guest? While writing in 1881 to her husband's nephew in Cöln, she recalled: "He was one of the handsomest men I ever saw—of light complexion, blue eyes, brown hair—elegant in manner and carriage—well read and full of humor, consequently was the life of any company. He was highly esteemed by men of letters and counted many men of ability among his friends."

The visitor's impressions of the Benson family appear in the next segment of his journal.

Thursday, April 28, 1836, on board the *Bee* on the
Mississippi. What a long intermission in my diary, caused by
suffering. From October 25th, when I wrote last, until a few
weeks ago, nothing but suffering, disease, and inconveniences
of all kinds; and the most horrible of all is that since last December I have been deprived of the use of my eyes. If I had been
able to write or to dictate, then I wouldn't have been so depressed mentally. Good Heavens! I would have been able to
describe all kinds of experiences with human beings at the
Steffelbachschen House. Now, with the use of only one eye, my
story must be postponed until later. Enough for now. My earnest desire to leave that miserable house was fulfilled, and I
breathe more freely in the open air.

At four o'clock this morning I left St. Louis aboard the *Bee*
en route to Peoria on the Illinois River in the state of Illinois.
We went upriver and, after a few hours, reached Alton on the
Illinois side. I cannot understand how anyone would build a
town on such a low part of the riverbank. Newly constructed
warehouses are presently under water, and in the streets (so far
I can see only one) the inhabitants are wading through water up
to their knees. With this and other disadvantages, Alton tries to
compete with St. Louis commercially. Since the latter is much

better located, it is *ridiculous.* Near the town the bank is rocky and in the distance are hills. The setting sun was on the water when we reached the 100-year-old French village of Portage des Sioux, inhabited only by Frenchmen who speak their own language and follow their own traditions.

April 29.   *Accidents in the West are very commonplace. We had proceeded only a few miles up the Illinois River last night, and everyone was gathered for a social hour in the cabin, when a blast was heard in the engine room, followed by hysterical screaming of the women passengers. Everyone was running around, and we thought the steam boiler had burst. Luckily it was only a cylinder that was damaged. One woman was injured on her chest and arm. The boats on the smaller rivers are mostly bad, but this is one of the better ones. The negligence in management of these river steamers is demonstrated by the fact that there was no yawl aboard in order to reach shore in emergencies. A few boards hastily nailed together as a raft served the purpose. If the accident had happened a few hours earlier on the Mississippi, where the current in springtime is very swift, this makeshift lifeboat would have been inadequate. Here we are now, tied to a tree on the bank, waiting for another boat that will be kind enough to carry us on our way. This finally happened on the 30th, and everyone scrambled on board the Helen Mar. What congestion on this steamboat! Sixty passengers added to thirty in a cabin hardly big enough* for eighteen! The first spot on this river to attract my attention is the so-called point where a few hills rise above the bottom land and a few small huts are visible. On the whole, the banks of the Illinois are flat and without charm.

Toward Noon, April 30. Where Apple Creek runs into the Illinois there is a beautiful bend, enclosed on one side by hills on which are two or three log houses. It was pretty crowded during the meal today. Seventy-five people had to be fed, and there was barely room for twenty.

Sunrise, May 1. What a night! In the narrow confines of the cabin they squeezed in fifty people. The whole floor was covered with sleepers. One could hardly step forward or backward. In Naples—yes, *Naples!!* I walked for a few hours last night, not surrounded by the shadows of gray antiques illuminated by Italian moonbeams, but near a dirty grocery where the new Neapolitans drank their whiskey and made rough jokes. This Naples has existed for ten years, but has not developed because of its unhealthy location, as with many of these Western settlements. For this reason, new towns are founded all the time. As soon as you set foot on shore someone hands you a notice of lots for sale, describing the various advantages of the location such as health, view, and other features. Now I am writing in the upper room of the helmsman, from where I can see Beardstown. Here I saw the following boat schedule on the wall:

Office Steamboat *Helen Mar*
Trip 18 Stoppages (as far as the Illinois is navigable)

Meachums	Beards Landing	Rome
Bushnells	Havana	Allenton
Neaples	Copper Creek	Columbia
Meredocia	Peking	Hennepin
Beardstown	Peoria	Ottawa

To the p[i]lots
Clk (Clerk)

The underlined names are towns; the others are merely landing places named for the owners who live nearby.

May 16.   Again, fourteen days have passed in suffering! Not far from Peking my eyes became much worse, so I had to remain in the cabin, and in this suffering condition I landed 24 hours later in Peoria. I was escorted to a guesthouse where I spent a whole day and a night. As elsewhere, I couldn't sleep because of bugs, even though I put my bedding on the floor. Not to mention the miserable food at the table, where only bad pork and other undigestible stuff was served; I have learned to live without good food and clean beds. The young Englishman whose acquaintance I made in the house of Mr. Flower at Albion had invited me last summer to visit him. His invitation was helpful now, in my pitiful circumstances. Therefore, I wrote him a few lines to tell him of my arrival and my condition. The next day, toward evening, he came in his wagon to pick me up. Here I am now, on the farm of the Benson family, very friendly and good-hearted people. But how this family lives and what hardships they have endured during their two years in America! Mr. Benson, the father, tempted by the brilliant descriptions of American life in the West as related to him by a man named Stuart, left England with his wife and six children, three sons and three daughters.

The children were well brought up in city life, in particular the two eldest sons and the eldest daughter, the latter an extremely charming Englishwoman whose careful education fitted her for life in the best London society. Mr. Benson left his family in Buffalo and traveled through the Western states in search of a suitable site for a farm. After searching here and there, he decided to settle on a big prairie near Peoria. It was Congress land, which he acquired by claim. He then fetched his family, which, after arrival, had to live in a common log cabin until the frame house he was building for them was completed. Being a foreigner and unfamiliar with American customs, his construction of the house was a failure from the very beginning. He was sold faulty materials, and the workmanship on the house was poor. Everything had to be hauled a great distance, which was expensive. When the house was half finished the family moved in. As the English style of living was about to begin, one hardship after another occurred.

After they had lived in the house a few weeks, the father came home from hunting with a double-barreled gun in his hand. A detonation was heard, then a rolling noise on the floor near the entrance to the house. Mother and daughter hurried to the scene. Oh horrible sight! The beloved husband, the dear father lay on the floor, bathed in his own blood. No sound was heard from him. He had stepped into the Eternal Life. What lamentation! The desolate mother and children standing around the body of the beloved father.[22] Later on, the mother became ill. She had never been happy there, but had hidden her grief for the sake of her husband and the children. Now, in the depths of despair, the mother grew steadily worse and no doctor was available. Finally, she decided to return with the girls to England, and they reached New York safely, having sold most of their personal property by public auction in St. Louis. In New York the mother died of a broken heart. The girls then rejoined their brothers on the farm near Peoria, their money gone. The impoverished orphans sought help from their relatives in England, but no help was offered, since English pride is devoid of sympathy. At the moment they are living on the farm under the motherly care of the eldest daughter, an angel of a woman, supported by a small amount of money received from England every month. Clad in deep mourning, they still cry over the loss of father and mother.

May 17.   After my long illness in St. Louis, which forced me to remain indoors all winter, it would have been very stimulating for me to enjoy the wholesome country air, but the climate here is so harsh that it is impossible to stay outdoors. Here I live on the huge flat prairie, vast as the ocean. The glaring sun is nowhere interrupted by shade trees, and there are no hills

---

[22] There is no suggestion here or in any other records that the elder John Benson's death was not accidental. Catastrophes of this nature were not uncommon on the frontier. Unlike most of the German emigrants, Benson had owned and cultivated his own land in the vicinity of Thorne, Yorkshire, in addition to practicing law in London. Financial losses forced him to seek a new life for himself and family in America in 1833. He was born on March 11, 1783, in Thorne, the son of John and Ann Atkinson Benson. He married Harriet Coupland of Doncaster on September 21, 1812. The accident the visitor describes here occurred on December 4, 1834.

to furnish protection against the wind, which blows endlessly. There is a sparse wooded area not far from here and a few clear springs that cannot be approached by human beings because of swarms of mosquitoes and many deadly rattlesnakes.

Speaking of privation, we have absolutely nothing and have to do without everything. Bad bacon, poor bread baked in an iron kettle and only half done, some tea morning and evening. The greatest luxury is some cheese now and then and a tasteless pudding at noon. Milk is the main food for these people, and I often admire my Englishwoman when I see how she eats like a sparrow. Tea and a piece of bread, bread and a little tea! In deference to me as a guest, friend, and stranger, I see at breakfast two eggs, of which, out of politeness, I dare eat only one. Sadly I watch the second egg being carried away. And so lives not only this family, but others. How the men, who have to work in the fields under the hot sun, can live on such scanty fare the Lord only knows.

May 19.   Riding in company of my Englishwoman and a friend to Peoria.[23] This town of 1,200 inhabitants has existed for five or six years. There are only two streets—*Water and Main.* Other streets are found only on the projected plan of the town. The houses, with very few exceptions, are primitive and contain only one or two rooms. Already there are 15 stores and a goodly number of taverns, of which the *Peoria Light House* is the most fashionable. Europeans think that the West is the newest of the New World and expect to find here the best man-

---

[23] The visitor's reluctance to mention Harriet Benson by name suggests an unwillingness at this time to acknowledge more than a casual interest in her.

ners, morals, and customs, but, to the contrary, these new frontier towns attract the excrement from the older cities of the East. Wherever a town is founded, groceries and taverns sprout like mushrooms from the ground. Lots and acreage are sold at high prices. On Jones Prairie, eight miles from town, all land except the military tracts is already in the hands of speculators. This prevents others from building homes and developing farms, and for this reason there are very few settlements to be found. To buy land at the Government price, one must go up-river to Ottawa or even as far as the Fox River.

On our way back home we visited an Englishman, Captain [Henry W.] Jones. Here I found a very brave family and excellent tea was served. We were offered fresh meat, tasty radishes, and nicely prepared eggs—a luxurious meal indeed! The farm of this hospitable Englishman stands also in the open prairie, but it has the advantage of a few beautiful bluffs behind the house, with very good bottom land between. Only a few fields are cultivated, the remainder being in their original state. His house, although small, is built in good taste.[24] How different from those miserable log cabins of the emigrated Americans. When the tea table was set, I thought I was in London or Paris. Exquisite porcelain, beautifully polished silverware on a white tablecloth, a large, handsome samovar, and other extra things that add to the comforts of life and are indispensable to the cultured European. This Englishman lives on an income, without which he would be unable to exist. By thrift and rigid economies, he can live much better here than he could in England

---

[24] An old two-story limestone house, possibly successor to the one in which the Bensons' guest was entertained so hospitably in 1836, was standing in 1964, unoccupied and in disrepair, on the north side of the Farmington Road, near the intersection with Maxwell Road in Limestone Township.

on the same amount of money. The eldest son works very hard in the fields, which yield only potatoes and a little corn.

May 20. How differently my English family lives from those in England. The eldest daughter, about 22 years, cannot get adjusted to this kind of life. She seldom complains, but the lines of grief are plainly visible in her features. The youngest daughter, about 17, seems to fit better into this life of lamentation. Religion, or rather the firm belief in God the Father, Son, and Holy Ghost, sustains them. They are Episcopalians who believe that they will find their eventual Paradise in Heaven. In the morning, right after breakfast, a chapter from the Bible is read; then everyone kneels while the eldest son reads the prayers of the church in a loud voice, always ending with the words: "The Grace of our Lord Jesus Christ, the love of God, and the fellowship of the Holy Ghost be with us all evermore, Amen."[25] But with all these prayers, which take place morning, noon, and night, the eldest daughter is not at all satisfied, and she reads during the day from the New Testament. Prayer is everything to her, and she thinks and speaks always of it. Often deep in thought, her head supported by her hand, I have heard her praying in a low voice. Frequently she would say to her sister: "Oh, that we could go to church next Sunday." You poor, good child, how modest are your desires!

The brothers go to their work in the fields and the sisters to their domestic duties, which are very primitive. Since they have no kitchen, they cook in the open, where the smoke and flame

---

[25] The younger John Benson was ordained as a priest of the Episcopal Church at Peoria in 1858 and became the first permanent rector of Christ Church, Limestone Prairie, which had been dedicated in 1845 by Bishop Philander Chase, the founder of Kenyon College in Ohio. The college was named in honor of Lord Kenyon, one of the original English donors to the church building fund. John Benson, his brother-in-law James Clark, and his wife's niece Isabella Douglass, donated twenty acres of land across the road from Christ Church *in glebe,* an English custom to supplement a clergyman's income. When the church was inactive during the depression of the early 1930's

blow in their faces. When they bake bread in an iron pot it often is not done. For their laundry, they carry water a half mile to the house from the nearest spring, in a ravine. In bad weather, cooking is done in the living room over a fire in the fireplace, which does not draw properly. At noon everyone gathers hungrily for a meal of bacon, bread, milk, and water in great quantity. The pudding on which the sisters worked all morning is a disappointment; nevertheless they eat it all. I always tried to comfort her by eating some of it and assuring her it was very tasty. Now the sons return to their work and the sisters busy themselves with the cleaning of the dishes and the silver; when this is done, they start mending their brothers' trousers. So time passes toward evening, when teatime approaches and the kettle is put on the fire. Now the trials of my Englishwoman begin again. The kettle, resting on the burning wood, is frequently upset, and once the entire contents were spilled on the Turkish rug. Thus, supper is delayed, but all hands are helping. The table is not loaded with food, but rather with dishes and silverware, suggesting what might have been served had it been available. Three kinds of bread—dry, spread, and toasted—are eaten with typical English formality. Each asks the others what he can do to help. Then come prayers again, after which everyone retires, exhausted from the labors of the day. And so passes day after day.

May 21. Here on this prairie also are many settlers from Kentucky and Tennessee. Believe it or not, they are pre-

---

this land was leased for a little more than $100 per year in perpetuity for agricultural purposes. Since 1964 legal measures to terminate this contract have been in process.

paring to move farther to the West. An American feels no particular attachment to the soil he cultivates. He makes a few improvements and then sells his farm to the first person who comes along with a good price, and that is why they are starting to move again. Someone mentions a new piece of land, regardless of its distance, which offers the advantages of good timber and fertile soil, or perhaps the opportunity of opening a store for trading or swapping, or founding a new town, and at once he hitches the oxen to his wagon, loads his wife and children and all his belongings, and starts moving. As before, he eats his bacon, drinks his bad tea, sleeps in his wagon, until he has found a new location that suits his taste. There he builds another log cabin and within a few days he already feels completely at home. For instance, yesterday I spoke to a few of these Americans, one of whom was heading for the headwaters of the Spoon River; another was on his way to the Fox River; a third man told me that "plenty of first-rate land and heaps of money" can be found on the Iowa River in Missouri, and he is going there. Everybody is talking of the many advantages of that place; but who can stand this nomadic life if he is not used to it from the beginning?

Sunday, May 22. Church and prayers, which words are constantly on the lips of my Englishwoman, prompted a ride to town and church this very day. A big four-wheeled wagon was loaded with chairs; my Englishwoman and I went on horseback; and so the cavalcade proceeded to town. On arrival, we were told there was no church service in the morning, but in the afternoon. We went to see a storekeeper named Grey, a deaf Irishman, where we obtained bread, butter, and a pie. For purely pious reasons, nobody cooks on Sunday. About two o'clock we went to church in a hard rain. A small, pitiful schoolhouse has to serve for this purpose. After waiting vainly for the minister to show up, I excused myself and went to see a German baker who runs a grocery. After reading an old German newspaper and listening to the conversation of a few dilettante German farmers, I returned to my company at the schoolhouse, where preparations already were being made to go home. On our way we again visited the hospitable Mr. Jones, where a tremendous dinner was awaiting us. I ate like a wolf, having had nothing more than bread and bacon for several days. Here we remained until sunset, and Mr. Jones helped pass the time during the pouring rain by recounting anecdotes of the Battle of Waterloo, where he had fought as a captain with the English dragoons. Going home, we tried to ford the Kickapoo River, which was swollen from the heavy rain. I and another man had to get out of the wagon and climb over a tree that had fallen into the water. Because of the darkness and my poor eyesight, I was momentarily in danger of falling into the stream, but luckily I reached the opposite bank, wet but unharmed, and we continued our journey. I worried constantly lest I break an arm or a leg on that terrible hay wagon. On our arrival at the farm, I felt dead tired from the church-going pleasure trip. The whole family was exhausted, and after saying a few prayers, we all went to bed.

May 24. We sit indoors in front of a big fire in the fireplace as if it were the month of January. What climate on these huge prairies, swept by the four winds! It penetrates to the marrow of your bones. I chopped wood to warm myself. I realize now that, because of the poor food, my resistance is low and I am lacking in energy. I can understand why the poor immigrants, who were used to a better life, reached for the whiskey bottle as a stimulant. In this house there is not a drop of this American stimulant because my English family is too God-fearing, or they must be members of a temperance society. Pure, clear well water is what we drink here. I have to smile when at times my charming Englishwoman offers me a glass of fresh water as a special favor. The people of the West seem to agree with the poet, Seume, who praises the virtues of pure water.[26] If one visits a log cabin, a drink of water is offered at once out of a calabash, and your host says: "Stranger, will you have a drink of water?" In the beginning I used to ask for a glass of water, but everybody stared at me, so now I ask for a drink.

July 1. Still suffering from my eye trouble, I made up my mind several days ago to leave this big, tiresome, shapeless prairie and the nearby Peoria with its 1,200 inhabitants in order to return to St. Louis.

---

[26] Johann Gottfried Seume (1763–1810), German writer best known for his *Walk to Syracuse*.

July 2. Here, waiting for the steamboat, I had an opportunity to observe the town and its inhabitants more closely. Never before have I seen such a rabble in beautiful clothing. Once they sight a stranger who is said to have a little money, they hunt him down and in a clandestine manner offer all kinds of real estate for sale—quarter sections, very well located, and town lots, to be subdivided at huge profits. It is like the bourse in Vienna and Frankfurt am Main, where people by the thousands carry on trade without having a dime in their pockets. People are referred to as being very rich when they have bonds or deeds to a few town lots. Just as the dear Frankfurters have nothing on their minds but metals, here in the West they talk of nothing but town lots. Out of ten people here, you can be sure that nine of them have one or more bonds or deeds for town lots in their pockets. Such lots are sold on credit, to be paid for in three, six, or twelve months. The buyer gets a bond that is exchanged for a deed when payment is made. By the time payment is due, the lot is sold to someone else at a higher price. If he cannot sell to his advantage and is unable to make payment, the owner takes off, and the lot is sold at auction. Such speculation in land is not good for a newly founded, growing town, because no one would think of building houses on lots that are bought and sold in such a manner, and therefore it is not unusual to see a flagstaff in the center of all the sold lots, with no buildings in sight. How else would anyone know that there is a town in that open prairie? The owner of a tavern sold it and the lot on which it stood, for 20,000 dollars, under the

---

condition that the buyer pay off a few hundred annually, and in case he is unable to complete his payment, the property will revert to the original owner. The advantage to the seller in such a speculative transaction is obvious. The tavern owner was one of the big proprietors of lots. When the news of this particular transaction spread through the town, many people rushed to buy lots before it was too late, and therefore the tavern owner sold his remaining lots at a high price. During my stay here, people talked of nothing but town lots and the rich German from Strasbourg who bought many of them in a gigantic swindle, hoping to become rich fast.

July 3. At two o'clock in the morning I left Peoria on board the steamboat *Liberty* for St. Louis. Where the Illinois enters the Mississippi, I saw the romantically located town of Grafton. What a pleasant sight after my monotonous stay on the prairies. It is a relief to see hills and valleys again, blended with forests and meadows.

Despite the pleasure he derived from the warmth of the Bensons' hospitality, still suffering from his eye ailment, the traveler was impatient after six weeks "to leave this big, tiresome, shapeless prairie and the nearby Peoria with its 1,200 inhabitants" and return to the more lively environment of St. Louis. As his river boat passed "the romantically located" town of Grafton at the confluence of the Illinois and Mississippi rivers, he made this entry in the journal, under date of July 3, 1836: "What a pleasant sight after my monotonous stay on the prairies. It is a relief to see hills and valleys again, blended with forests and meadows." But the bedbugs, dirt, and other inconveniences of his new boardinghouse, for which he paid five dollars per week, and the "pestilent summer air of St. Louis" prompted the itinerant to embark upon another venture, this time a visit to the German settlement at Belleville, seventeen miles southeast of the city, in Illinois.

Here he stayed about two weeks in a guesthouse, from which he could "stroll in all directions through the village," inspecting its buildings and picking up information about its inhabitants, especially those of German origin. Accompanied by a resident of the Duden settlement in Missouri, he visited several German farmers on the outskirts of Belleville, observed their circumstances, and listened sympathetically to their complaints. In Belleville, as in Peoria, there was much excitement among the people over the founding of new towns and the speculation in town lots.

Here is the record of his findings, as reflected in the diary:

Belleville, July 16, 1836. 17 miles from St. Louis. In the Hopkins boardinghouse in St. Louis, where I sought shelter after my return from Peoria, and where there were bedbugs, dirt, and inconveniences of all kinds, for which I had to pay five dollars per week, I stayed only one week; then came here to Belleville, partly to flee the pestilent summer air of St. Louis, and partly because I wanted to see with my own eyes this place which is highly praised by Frankfurters and Rhinelanders on account of its German settlement. I have been here six days in a guesthouse, from which I can stroll in all directions through the village. Belleville is located on a nameless muddy creek, surrounded by small woods and a few prairies. It has well-built brick houses and several frame structures as well as a courthouse with two wooden pillars. There is a haughty and arrogant German lawyer here who was a councilor of war in Frankfurt am Main and even participated in the Frankfurt "storm in a bottle." Because of his title and the money he brought with him from Germany, he carries his nose very high and lives with his nieces and nephews in a charming brick house.[27]

There are many groceries here and one German storekeeper who has made a great deal of money. There is also a brewery here, opened recently by two Germans, several steam and water mills, and a distillery owned by a cousin of the councilor of war and another German.[28] Yesterday I went with Mr. Rafauf, who lives in the Duden settlement in Missouri, to visit German farmers in the environs of Belleville. We started in the direction of the so-called Turkey Hill, and on our way we visited the

---

[27] This reference is applicable to no Belleville resident at the time of Gustorf's visit and obviously came from unreliable sources. Gustav Körner, a participant in the Frankfurt Attentat who, with several of his co-conspirators settled in Belleville after escaping from Germany, was enjoying his honeymoon when Gustorf arrived there. The occupant of the house he mentions was Theodor Erasmus Hilgard, former secretary of the Palatinate and a supreme court justice in his native land, who emigrated with his wife and nine children (not nieces and nephews) in 1834; although many of his friends, including Körner and Engelmann, were political refugees, Hilgard's decision to emigrate may have resulted from his failure to be appointed professor of law at a Bavarian university.
[28] This was Edward Hilgard who, with a farmer named Fritz Wolf, owned

home of Mr. Hilgard, where a brave, hospitable woman served us a drink of apple wine. During our conversation she talked very praiseworthily about the German social life in Illinois, in contrast to the German social life in Missouri. However, I have my doubts about the truth of her statements if Belleville Germans like the arrogant lawyer and the still operator are considered typical examples of the German settlers in Illinois. Does she refer to prosperous and related families who visit each other on Sundays, drinking coffee within the family circle and reminiscing about the past? If so, then she is right.

These people own a beautiful, well-furnished, and roomy house surrounded by a romantically located farm. But what use are things when health is poor? The head of the family is ill with fever.

A few miles farther, over a brush-covered prairie and on the edge of a wood, we visited Baron Haxthausen.[29] Here everything was weather-beaten and gone to seed—a true sow's life, as the doctor at St. Charles would have called it. The poor Baron, here only a year, had too many irons in the fire at once; beside the farm, he had a small and ill-equipped distillery, and now he is building a mill. He is unmarried, has four laborers, and a peasant woman with children to keep house for him. We had a very poor lunch, prepared by the Baron himself because his housekeeper was in bed with the fever. We then visited several other farms, German as well as American, all of them prosperous so long as the people did the work themselves and didn't have to depend upon hired help. In other words, those who are

---

and operated a distillery in West Belleville.

[29] Hermann and Henry von Haxthausen of Westphalia bought a farm about a mile south of Theodor Engelmann. The visitor apparently was unaware of the existence of a brother.

used to farm work from their youth are successful, whether they work their own farms or rent a piece of land. The wealthy Germans, to be successful farmers, must obtain experienced peasant tenants. Only in this way can they hold their own. To this group belong the families of Reis [Reus], Schott, and Engelmann.[30] Everywhere we went on our way home, American farmers offered their land for sale at speculative prices. Speculation in land has become a pestilence throughout the West. They want ten to twenty dollars per acre, depending upon "improvements" and location. One American, who praised his soil to high Heaven, told me that "the Germans intend to have the entire county (St. Clair) to themselves, and that is the reason why we want to move on." I smiled and went on my way, but had to promise to visit him in order to admire his property.

July 18. Belleville has indeed the most beautiful wooded walks I have seen so far in Illinois. With a Doctor Tiensch, who recently began practicing medicine here, I walked along the Kaskaskia road through the woods. On the left, near town, I saw a farm that belongs to Mr. Crane. It is the most beautiful farm I have seen, so far as general appearance of land and buildings is concerned. The location is very romantic; the farmhouse stands on rising ground, surrounded by cultivated fields, orchards, and meadows; there are six hundred fruit trees; the livestock appeared to be healthy. For the first time I thought: This is the perfect farm life. Mr. Crane has busied himself for twenty years with the improvements on his farm, and

---

[30] Adolph Reus was a medical practitioner from Frankfurt; Anton Schott, Ph.D., who studied philosophy at Jena and Halle, was a professor of history at the Frankfurt Gymnasium; he established the first public library in Belleville, now the oldest in Illinois.

one can see that everything is arranged efficiently and with good taste. Yesterday I met a farmer named [Fritz] Wolf who lives six to eight miles from here. He did not seem to be very enthusiastic over the produce from his land. If you inquire openly, one seldom gets the facts. But if one uses an indirect approach, then the situation comes to light in its true colors. For example, I said: "Since your farm is near St. Louis, a good market for your products, you must be doing very well." The answer: "Good Heavens, how mistaken you are! To drive to the market and sleep in the wagon, like the Americans, is out of the question. To spend money on a guesthouse is too expensive. I would rather stay on my farm and give my corn to the livestock." So I said: "Well, then you can sell the pigs you have fed and make a lot of money." He replied: "Those we eat ourselves." "Then you have a very easy life," I suggested. "A beautiful life," he exclaimed, "when you add 200 dollars a year to the farm!" I asked him if he had been a farmer in Germany. His answer was no, and I had had enough.

July 27.   In St. Louis. On the 26th I left Belleville in order to receive letters I was expecting in St. Louis. Here I want to mention that in Belleville and vicinity, people talk about nothing but the founding of new towns and the purchase of town lots. A town recently founded by a lawyer near Occa [sic] or Kaskaskia was named Tamarawa; another town, founded by someone else, has the Scottish name of Waverly, and the handbill advertising town lots reads as follows:

Sale of Lots in the Town of
Waverly

This town is on the main road from St. Louis to Shawneetown, and on the Railroad route from the latter place to Alton in Washington County, Illinois, about 15 miles west from Nashville, the Seat of Justice of said County, 20 miles east of Bellville, eighteen South East of Lebanon, 25 South of Carlyle, and five east of the Kaskaskia river.

Waverly.

is situated in a high rolling beautiful prairie, surrounded by some of the finest groves of timber, sufficient for every purpose, and inexhaustible beds of stone coal and quarries of rock are in the vicinity.

The rapidly augmenting population of the country seems to demand the location of a town at this place. The settlements now established are composed of enterprising and industrious farmers, and the certainty of the improvement of the navigation of the Kaskaskia river, with the advantages to be derived from the rail road, warrants the belief that Waverly must soon become a point of considerable business, and a desirable and safe place for the investment of capital.

It is well known that the County of Washington can scarcely be excelled in point of fertility and agricultural advantages, and the public improvements now in contemplation will direct public attention to a section of country that can no longer escape the attention of men of enterprise and capital.

Sale of Lots will take place:

on the premises on Saturday, the 6th day of August, on a credit
of 6, 12, and 18 months, the purchaser giving notes with approved
security.

W. Pensoneau

J. J. Chandler

Waverly, July 23, 1836   S. B. Chandler

I met a very original Englishman in Belleville; his name was
Boscott. He seemed to be a very cultured man, having studied
theology at Oxford, traveled through most of the European
Continent, and lived in the southern part of France, whence he
came to the Western states of America. Hearing of the easy
and gracious way of farming in America, he made up his mind
precipitately to become an American farmer. He came here
two or three years ago, bought 240 acres of Government land,
lives in a shabby log cabin, and cultivates the soil. But now he
regrets his decision for the same reasons I have mentioned
previously, and he is looking forward to selling his farm in order
to return to southern France. There he can live as a gentleman
for 300 dollars, whereas here he lives a miserable life, devoid of
luxuries. He was not the type who starts something in a super-
ficial manner; to the contrary, he went right to work with zeal
and by early this year had, by himself, cultivated 96 acres of
prairie and fenced 100 acres. He estimates the present value of
his farm as up to 2,500 dollars, but would be glad to sell for
2,000 in order to end his "life of misery and vexation of spirit."

Boscott has a strong antipathy toward the Methodists because of their religious intolerance and their bad influence over those people whose lives are filled with uncertainty and superstition. He also talked of the local practice of going to court over the most trivial disputes and the tendency of the courts to rule against strangers, particularly European immigrants. By the way, this man was very entertaining and was fond of jokes, which the English people call "humor." For instance, one day Doctor Tiensch, who belongs to the long-suffering, complaining, regretting class of Germans, passed us with sorrowful glance and stooped posture, dragging behind him his small, neglected boy. He [Boscott] said: "The doctor looks like patience upon a monument smiling at grief."

July 28.   Upon arrival in St. Louis with plans to stay for a while, one must face the problem of finding a suitable place to live. The boardinghouses are bad, expensive, and always filled to capacity. The hotels are 50 dollars a month and are no better than the cheap taverns. Not knowing where to turn, the Germans take refuge at Staffelbach's boardinghouse, where you have to live like pigs in a stable except for the food. Never having tried Clopicki's boardinghouse, I went there and was offered a room—or call it a dirty hole—where I could sleep alone (a great privilege in this country). Above me, in a still shabbier hole, sort of an attic, were several Poles, with which this house was swarming, and they slept on the floor. In the evening, when I wanted to go to bed in this Polish mess, I was told by the owner (ad-

dressed by the Americans as General, Major, or Baron) that my
bed was already occupied by two Americans who had been
guests on a previous occasion and had returned unexpectedly,
and therefore I would have to sleep on the sofa. But what a
night! Bedbugs and millions of mosquitoes gnawed me half to
death. The Poles kept running in and out of the room; then the
Americans came, wanting something to drink. One man, complaining of the mosquitoes, was running around in his night-
shirt. The Major, himself, who slept on a few chairs in the court
under the open sky, didn't care in the least what was going on
inside the house. Now and then he raised up from his chairs
and spoke a few Polish, German, French, and now and then
English words, depending upon the language in which he was
addressed. Clopicki is a man of dignified demeanor, his behavior being that of an old French émigré. As badly as he speaks
German and English, his French is perfect. The meals were
pretty good, particularly at noon when the proprietor sat at the
head of the table and everything was *piano pianissimo*, the first
time in two years that I saw people eating decently and without
the slightest confusion (Americans habitually shovel the food
into their mouths as rapidly as possible). The meals were served
as in Germany and France, one course after another, with in-
tervals between. When I was ready to retire the second night,
my sofa was occupied by card players and drunkards, and since
I didn't want to stay up late, I went to the hole that had been
offered to me originally, but it was like jumping from the frying
pan into the fire because the bed was infested with bugs, mos-

quitoes, and Polish fleas. Taking shelter in Hell couldn't have been worse. At two in the morning, a German wedding party arrived—doctors, lawyers, and students. They made a lot of noise until dawn and then left the house.

August 4.   On this day I left the Polish-German-French-American grocery of Mr. Clopicki, so-called because here is a true Babylon of languages; nevertheless, the most prevailing one was Polish. Here is the center or rather the hangout of all the St. Louis Poles. On the whole, they appear to be very pitiful and long-suffering, but the majority of them retain most of their native vivacity and enthusiasm. For instance, they gathered here one evening to drink beer and sing their Polish national songs. They seem to be cheerful but only in a half-hearted way. Unlike the German, the Pole does not readily forget his mother country, and therefore it is hard for him to adjust to foreigners, especially when they are as cold as the Americans.

Confusion apparently existed in Gustorf's mind regarding the identity and status of two people he mentions somewhat casually in his journal, the distinguished Belleville citizens Theodor Erasmus Hilgard and Gustave Koerner.

Hilgard was one of the early gentlemen farmers popularly referred to as the "Latin Peasants." He was born July 7, 1790, in the Rhenish Palatinate. While a student at Göttingen University he submitted a poem to Goethe for criticism. Hilgard established himself as a lawyer at Trier at age twenty-one; subsequently he lived in Kaiserslautern and Zweibrücken. He and his first wife, Gretchen Pauli, had five daughters and four sons. Hilgard became secretary of the Palatinate Parliament in 1821 and a supreme court justice in 1826. At the height of an apparently successful professional career, he emigrated in the fall of 1835, arriving in Belleville with his large family on February 23, 1836. There he purchased a farm that subsequently became the nucleus of West Belleville. Mrs. Hilgard died in 1842, one year after her husband became an American citizen. Twelve years later the sixty-four-year-old widower married his twenty-five-year-old niece.

Hilgard died in Heidelberg in 1865, having crossed the Atlantic eight times. (Helmut Hirsch, "Theodor Erasmus Hilgard," *Journal of the Illinois State Historical Society*, Vol. 37, No. 2 [June, 1944], 164–72.) Koerner described Theodor Hilgard at age forty-six as "close in all money matters . . . loved his family, no doubt, but he loved himself more. His comfort, his well-being, was his principal care." (Koerner [Körner], *Memoirs*, 388.) This would have been 1836, the year of Hilgard's arrival in Belleville and of Gustorf's visit to the area.

It is unfortunate that Gustorf was unable to meet and talk with Judge Hilgard, whom he seemingly derides. Had the Judge's indisposition not prevented such a confrontation, the record undoubtedly would have been clarified so far as Gustorf's comments regarding the jurist's political activities in Germany were concerned. Although his somewhat precipitate departure for the United States suggests a personal crisis of some kind, there is nothing in the record to indicate that the move was politically motivated.

With Gustave Koerner, however, the circumstances were quite different. On October 18, 1835, in St. Louis, the diarist had commented upon a pamphlet written by Koerner in Belleville and printed in Germany, which was critical of Gottfried Duden. Gustorf felt that the writer "withholds many facts which, for reasons of his own, are not revealed in his pamphlet. He should speak freely, if his real purpose is to be of help to his countrymen." During his visit to Belleville, therefore, it is natural to assume that the traveler would have made an earnest effort to meet and talk with the pamphlet's author. If such a meeting took place, it is not recorded in the diary, nor is there any further reference to the pamphleteer by name.

Gustave Koerner, the fugitive from the Frankfurt uprising, who was unmarried, and a number of other fugitives with their families, had emigrated to the United States in 1833 from Le Havre. Having settled initially at Shiloh, about six miles east of Belleville, and studied law in Lexington, Kentucky, for about two years, Koerner was admitted to the Illinois Bar by the Supreme Court at Vandalia, and in June, 1835, he entered into a law partnership with Adam W. Snyder, whose office was on the public square of Belleville. In June of the following year, Koerner married Sophie Engelmann, sister of his friend and former co-conspirator, Theodor. Gustorf visited Belleville in July of the same year, when the bride and groom probably were still on their honeymoon, which would explain why he recorded no interview with the man who was destined to become Belleville's favorite son.

Although certain of Koerner's activities on behalf of German immigrants, as described later in his memoirs, reveal a lack of personal modesty that might properly be described as arrogance, *aloof* rather than *haughty* would be more appropriate in describing his bearing. Actually, the object of the diarist's obvious disdain was a nonentity, a fictional character created in his own mind from unidentified and obviously unreliable local sources and based upon the combined but not necessarily similar political backgrounds of Koerner and Judge Hilgard. Unfortunately, the diarist was unable to meet and talk with either man. Had he done so, the confusion in his mind regarding which of the two men had participated in revolutionary activities in Germany would have been clarified.

As a young lawyer in Frankfurt, a politically independent or "free" city, Koerner was admittedly a leader in a conspiracy whose purpose was not, as Frederick Julius wrote in his diary, to overthrow the authority of the King of Bavaria, but to combat a much more formidable political force, the German Confederation or *Deutscher Bund*. This organization of German states was established on June 6, 1815, during the Congress of Vienna and was not dissolved until 1866. Thirty-five dukes and the leaders of four free cities participated in the Bund, and Frankfurt am Main was its seat of government. The most active opposition to the Bund was provided by members of the politically oriented Burschenschaften or student associations, first organized in Jena in 1815 but dissolved by the Bund between 1819 and 1848 because of their radical and revolutionary political objectives.

Meanwhile, another revolutionary group, who called themselves the Press and Fatherland Society, was organized in 1832 with headquarters in Frankfurt and branches in several other western German cities. Society members, most of whom were merchants and professional men, joined forces with several of the suppressed but still politically active chapters of the Burschenschaften in an abortive and dramatically inept attack upon a military barracks near the Frankfurt Zeil on April 3, 1833. The incident, recorded historically as the "Frankfurter Attentat," had no immediate political impact upon the German Confederation, but the long-range effect upon its subjects was a major factor in the early economic development of southern Illinois and eastern Missouri.

Koerner was wounded in the ill-timed and poorly organized attack upon the barracks, which was attempted by a handful of the conspirators who relied more upon the psychological impact of their action than on fire power. Fortunately, the wound was not serious enough to prevent Koerner's escape from the city, disguised as a woman. With the help of friends, he fled Germany and made his way to a French port, a political fugitive with false papers.

He emigrated to Belleville, where his friend and former co-conspirator, Theodor Engelmann, had settled several years previously. The latter had escaped from Germany after being summoned for trial at Kaiserslautern on a charge of revolutionary activities. Traveling by stage on the road to Metz for a secret meeting with fellow conspirators, Koerner had recognized Engelmann, knapsack on his shoulders and walking along the side of the road. Contrary to the rules of the highway, Koerner ordered the stage driver to take his friend aboard. Thus learning of his friend's precarious situation, Koerner had been able to help him on the first step of his long flight

118

to freedom in America. The farm established by Engelmann near Belleville became a refuge for other political fugitives from Germany, including Koerner, who arrived in the fall of 1833. He was only twenty-four years of age, unmarried, and unaccompanied by any members of his family (Koerner, *Memoirs*, 217–42).

Gustave Koerner's political ambitions carried him as far as the office of Lieutenant Governor of Illinois. In Springfield, he met and became friendly with Abraham Lincoln, whose candidacy for President he supported vigorously, and who later appointed him United States Ambassador to Spain.[31]

Ten days after entering the Clopicki establishment the unhappy guest left "the hangout of all the St. Louis Poles" and boarded the elegant new river boat *Howard* for passage up the Missouri River to Washington, site of the Duden colony.

His first glimpse of the obscure town whose environs had been so widely publicized throughout Germany in Duden's extravagant account of the abundant opportunities awaiting the European immigrant on the western frontier should have been a source of great satisfaction to the man who had set out with so much confidence and enthusiasm from Philadelphia to inspect the colony and perhaps to join it. But circumstances, personal and social, had changed his view. He had lost much energy and resilience through illness; his physical condition and the disillusioning reports of the colony had dampened his enthusiasm. Few of the German immigrants he had talked with in St. Louis and its vicinity were willing or able to say anything good about Duden or his colony. Many of them reviled Duden for having, as they thought, fraudulently misrepresented living conditions and withheld information about the physical hardships of the frontier.

While staying in the English colony at Albion, Gustorf had tried to prepare himself for unaccustomed labor by working for a farmer during the harvest season without pay. He had thought, in this way, to gain practical experience in farming. Although he started with the easiest task, raking hay, and worked only two hours daily, he

---

[31] Additional information concerning the Frankfurt Attentat and its leadership is contained in an intensely interesting and informative study of the life of the young German rebel, Friedrich Adolph Wislizenus, by Douglas D. Hale, Jr., Associate Professor of History, Oklahoma State University, in the *Missouri Historical Review*, LXII, No. 3 (April, 1968), 260–85.

soon came to the conclusion that "the occupation of farming is almost impossible for an immigrant in this country, especially one who is physically unfit for this kind of work and therefore dependent upon others for help." Also, during his visit with the Benson family on Limestone Prairie he had helped with the spring planting, turned a small patch of earth near the house for a kitchen garden, chopped wood occasionally to keep warm, and performed other chores, but even these less strenuous tasks of farming had taxed his strength. His resistance was low, and the exertions quickly tired him. Perhaps realization of his inability to endure the vicissitudes of frontier life affected his impressions of Missouri, as recorded in his journal.

Trip on the Missouri River

On August 5th I went aboard the steamboat *Howard* where everything was elegant and newly installed, in order to travel up the Missouri. This boat goes all the way up to Fort Leavenworth, a distance of 500 miles, and has 80,000 silver dollars on board to be used in paying Indian annuities. The trip upstream takes six days; downstream, three. The fare upstream is 20 dollars and downstream, 15 dollars.

So far the only difference between the Missouri and the Mississippi is a more rapid current and more frequent bends. There is a great navigational hazard from the snags, and therefore the boat has to anchor at night until the moon rises. For the first time in eight days I slept peacefully. The bed was very good, clean, and furnished with a mosquito bar.

Afternoon. The farther one travels up the Missouri, the higher and more wooded the banks become. The scenery changes frequently from bluffs to bottom land. Also there are a few towering rocks. Such a phenomenon would attract little attention in Europe, but on these American rivers, where the scenery is usually very monotonous, each change is noticeable. The riverbanks are sparsely inhabited. The eye sees nothing but dense forests and fast-moving, muddy water; now and then a sand bar on which driftwood is accumulated; otherwise the same picture for 300 miles.

Point Pleasant. The captain said to me: "I am hunting for a town—ah, there it is!" And we approached a small hill on which stood two unfinished log cabins. To my great surprise, we unloaded a lot of merchandise for the store that occupied one of the log houses. This town has been in existence for only a few weeks, and for this reason the captain couldn't find it. The area is covered with trees except the spot where the future warehouse stands. About 20 farmers at the landing were very excited to see the first steamboat make a landing there. One farmer said: "Hear how she creaks and hisses." And his companion replied: "She is bursting!"

August 6. Washington on the Missouri was my destination, where I wanted to study the living conditions of the German settlers, so highly praised by Duden. Dusk was falling when we anchored at the new town of South Point, where there were again only two log houses. At first I thought this was my destination, but no, it was two miles farther. Then someone said: "Here is your town." It was almost dark when we anchored at Washington. I saw nothing but a wooded hill on which stood a few shabby log cabins. About 20 people stood on the bank, one with a long pipe in his mouth—a German! To him I turned, inquiring for Mr. [Charles] Iberius [sic], who had been recommended to me as a boardinghouse proprietor. But Mr. Iberius had no room for me, and another German offered room and board in his house. His name was [Bernard] Fricke. He came from Cassel and was a saddler by profession. Fricke led the way to his house, an unfinished frame structure completely open to the weather. I was offered a small room in which he and his family had been living. An American wouldn't have been so generous. Because of my ailing eye, he and his family moved into an unfinished room. I slept comfortably in a nice, clean bed. In the morning a girl came into my room to light the fire and make my coffee. I got out of bed and looked over the whole town of Washington for the first time. Six or eight houses stand on a wooded hill, and many trees have been cut to build additional houses. The inhabitants are Germans and Americans. My host is one of the earliest German settlers. He came here three years ago and was given this lot as a gift, on condition that he build a house on it. Then there are the Krüger brothers who manage a sort of medicine store. There is a storekeeper, also named Iberius [brother of Charles], a cabinetmaker, and a tanner. This is the entire population of the town, surrounded by the Duden colony. Peculiar circumstances hindered the development of Washington, which was founded by Mr. [William G.] Owens a few years ago. He was shot by another American, bringing the sale of lots to a standstill. According to the law, nothing can be sold until the youngest child comes of age; meanwhile, the houses may rot away or other towns may develop nearby.[32]

---

[32] Ralph Gregory, in his undated pamphlet *History of Washington, Missouri to the Civil War*, described William G. Owens and his wife Lucinda as native Kentuckians who moved to Missouri Territory in 1818, the year Franklin County was formally established. One year later Owens became the first postmaster of New Port, the county seat; by 1821 he had been appointed clerk of the county court. When it was decided that the county seat should be more centrally located for the convenience of all concerned, Owens, as one of two county commissioners, helped to survey a new county site to be known as Union. In the process of establishing the new county seat, both men surveyed and sold lots, and after the new courthouse was completed in Union, Owens bought and leased a considerable amount of land near Washington Landing, which he

Sunday, August 7. Since my arrival it has rained constantly, and, as in all these miserable places, one gets terribly bored if he cannot go outdoors. I spent my time in an unfinished brick house owned by four unmarried Germans. I read a few Hamburg newspapers while the owners played cards with the saddler and the cabinetmaker and drank cheap beer. The room was very disorderly. Dirty bedding was on the floor as well as trunks that served as chairs. On the wall hung pipes, student caps, guns, and German hunting trophies. One of the students, half naked, sat in a corner mending his pants, while another son of the Muse was busy repairing his boots. And so they sat, stood, or lay around the room when suddenly a horn sounded and the entire company proceeded to the saddler's house for the evening meal.

I also saw and talked today with Mr. [Louis] Abersmann [Eversmann] who is mentioned in the Duden book. He has been here since 1824, and if he did not have a German pipe in his mouth and had not spoken German, I would have thought he was a Kentuckian because of his Western American appearance. He held a long whip in his hand and talked about buying a few strong Negro slaves on the upper Missouri where he plans to go himself to get them. He invited me to share a bottle of whiskey which already he was enjoying.[33]

August 9. Yesterday was the day we wanted to inspect the lots in the projected town of Dortmund. For a long time it

believed to be a logical site for a county seat.

Owens bought one of the ferries at Washington Landing and fifty acres of land adjoining it for $650, and the first lots, probably surveyed by himself, were sold at public auction on July 4, 1829. Owens offered liberal terms to prospective buyers and is generally considered by local historians as the actual founder of the town of Washington. Both the town and its promoter appeared to have excellent prospects, but unfortunately he was shot in the back and killed by an unidentified assailant on November 16, 1834. This tragedy left the future of Washington uncertain and the victim's estate in a complicated legal tangle.

Four years later, John F. Mense, an astute and practical businessman, married Sarah, daughter of Lucinda and the late William G. Owens. With legal assis-

has been my desire to witness an auction in a newly developing
town. Dortmund was of particular interest to me because it was
[being] founded by a German. If one does not have a horse in
this part of the country he is just as badly off as a human being
without legs. The ground was very loose and muddy from the
downpour. Walking through it, the mud came practically up to
my knees. All my efforts to rent a horse were in vain, so I decided to go on foot. Accompanied by Mr. Fricke, to show me
the way, I started at eight o'clock in the morning. We crossed
the river by ferryboat, then along a road through wet bottom
land and dense woods. The trees were covered by creepers and
wild grape vines. To travel here by foot is very difficult because
of the humidity.

The road was not clearly defined, and it was necessary to pick
our way through tangled brush and swamps. We crossed a rain-
swollen creek on a fallen tree and climbed several high fences.
My guide finally led me to our destination, the farm of Mr.
[Julius] Malingrott [Mallinckrodt]. Before we reached it,
however, we visited the farms of the Messrs. Kinsel [sic], Bahre,
[Heinrich] von Martels, and Mumm [sic]. We went indoors
at the Von Martels farm. He was a young man of pleasant
manner and beautiful features. He wore a heavy beard on his
cheeks and a clipped mustache. I was received very kindly. His
clothes were those of a farmer, but his face was that of an aristocrat. Mr. von Martels fetched us a pail of water with which
we refreshed ourselves before continuing our journey.

---

tance from two St. Louis lawyers, Mense succeeded in untangling the affairs of
the deceased to the complete satisfaction of all concerned, thus officially establishing the town of Washington.

[33] Louis Eversmann, Duden's traveling companion from Germany to Missouri
in 1824, settled on land adjacent to the Duden farm on Lake Creek, north
of Washington. He did not return to Europe with Duden in 1827, but remained
in the settlement, adapted himself rapidly to American ways, married an
American woman, and became one of the first German immigrants to own
slaves. He died just before the Civil War, a slaveholder to the end. Gert Goebel,
Länger als ein Menschenleben in Missouri (C. Witter, Buchhandlung, St.
Louis, 1877), 6.

Toward noon we reached our objective, at the foot of a steep hill. We climbed the hill to the home of the founder of the new town. Forty or fifty riding horses were tethered in front of the house, and we later found out that we were the only ones who had come on foot. The only person in sight was a small girl, who told me that everybody had gone to town. "Where is the town?" I asked. "I don't know that myself," she replied. Suddenly a group of people approached the house; I followed them. The house stands on the top of a hill, with a majestic view of the Missouri River. The eye can follow the river for a great distance as it bends and winds through the forest. On the other side of the river there is a farm in the bottom land, the buildings looking very picturesque. But now it is time I mention the invisible town itself.

Mr. Malingrott [Mallinckrodt],[34] a tall, thin man and a true busybody in his manner, approached us. He looked over all the people, then said: "Gentlemen, let us start the sale of the lots." We all moved to the rear of the house, then to the woods where the sale was to take place. The area was full of people, most of them Germans, only a few well dressed, and many of them in rags.

At a table on which lay the town plan and other papers, sat a fat fellow, presumably the squire; next to him the clerk, the constable, and another official. Beside the table were two barrels, one filled with whiskey and the other with brandy. On another table, surrounded by benches, there were two or three glasses and a bucket of water. A Negro slave belonging to Mr.

---

[34] Julius, Emile, Herman, and Conrad Mallinckrodt emigrated to St. Charles County in 1833. Of the three brothers, Julius moved to St. Louis and by 1870 had become a wealthy industrialist. Herman and Conrad continued to cultivate their farms near Augusta, a town founded by an American named Harold and originally called Mount Pleasant.

Malingrott [Mallinckrodt] sat beside the barrels and kept the glasses filled; everyone had plenty to drink. The cultured people were enjoying themselves by telling jokes, but a group of peasants from Osnabrück, dressed in red striped jackets and blue overalls, began telling obscene stories. Osnabrücker are known here as Ossagen.

A few more serious-minded people were discussing past and future events. Among them was a Mr. [George] Münich [sic].[35] Suddenly the American auctioneer, standing on a chair, cried: "Silence, gentlemen!" He then started to read the conditions of the sale; then Mr. Münich stood on a chair and began to interpret what the auctioneer was saying, but he had difficulty, and so another German took over as interpreter. "How much is bid for a first-rate lot, number 54?" The aforementioned Ossagen, now thoroughly intoxicated from the whiskey, roared: "Ten, twenty, thirty dollars" until all lots were sold. With one exception, all the buyers were Ossagen. They were overjoyed to learn that they had a year to pay for the lots and could sell them for a profit.

Mr. Malingrott [Mallinckrodt], himself, was very busy with the sale, and it was amusing to hear him say that we were standing in the market place when actually we were surrounded by heavy woods. After the sale was over, we all went to the house where two hams, a big basket of bread, and whiskey were offered to the buyers and guests. Everybody helped themselves, and since there was little room around the table, they stretched out on the grass, eating the meat with their hands. In the room, not

---

[35] There is little doubt that this individual was George Münch, younger brother of Frederick Muench, ordained minister and leader of the second section of the Giessen Emigrant Society, who had settled immediately adjacent to the Duden farm in 1834 and was destined to become the spiritual and cultural leader of the colony. George emigrated later and settled near Augusta where he became a preacher, teacher, and skilled gunsmith. He and the Mallinckrodt brothers were neighbors. Unlike his elder brother Frederick, George apparently had not yet anglicized the spelling of the family name. William G. Bek on "The Followers of Duden," *Missouri Historical Review*, XVIII, No. 4 (July, 1924), 582.

far from the table, lay a man in a sickbed. His eyes were closed and he seemed to be in great pain, but nobody paid any attention to the poor devil. After the meal, everyone shook hands, mounted their horses, and started for home. The terrain of this embryo town is not of the best, and some say it is not in the least suitable for a town. Between two hills is a deep ravine in which the main part of the town is supposed to be.

Since the sale of lots, other difficulties have developed that will be to the town's disadvantage. For example, two Americans owning nearby farms have announced plans to establish towns on the river with docking facilities for boats, which the founder of Dortmund hasn't even thought of. Furthermore, there can be no ferry in Dortmund because there already is one in the neighboring town of Mount Pleasant. Also, the Americans have promised not to have one on the opposite bank. The founder of Dortmund has had an argument with his neighbors regarding the direction of the road between the towns. And the Americans already have a store in their town, which is a great advantage; and a grocery is being built. A German has promised to build a steam sawmill and a flour mill in Dortmund within five years, imagine! We Germans are great philosophers and theoreticians, but we are poorly equipped to compete with the Americans in commercial enterprises.[36]

August 11. After my walk through the woods I came to St. John's Creek, where I saw a mill, recently bought by Mr. [John William] Teppe [Tappe], two and a half miles from

---

[36] As the visitor predicted, the town of Dortmund, named after the Mallinckrodt brothers' birthplace east of Essen in the Kingdom of Westphalia, never got beyond the planning stage.

Washington. With the mill are 160 acres of land, so far uncul-
tivated. A farmer, [Daniel] McCoy, told me the location is very
unhealthy, which is the reason the former American owner sold
it. Mr. Teppe [Tappe] paid 2,000 dollars for the property, but
McCoy says it is hardly worth 1,000 dollars because in the spring
there is too strong a current on the river and in the summer
there is not enough.[37] On a small hill near a cornfield stands an
old, rotted log cabin in which I met a fat woman from Bielefeld
who was baking bread.

She has six children, two of them grown sons. One of the
children was in bed with an attack of the fever. Another child
was whimpering on the floor, and a third was on a German box,
crying. The woman offered me a drink of water and told me all
kinds of hard-luck stories concerning her trip from Germany:
First the inconveniences of the sea voyage; then the many hardships of the canal boats. She complained also about all the inconveniences she suffered in those bad St. Louis boardinghouses
while her husband was looking for a suitable place to live.

She asked me if I believe the Americans have religion. Certainly, I replied; they have many churches and all belong to
some religious sect. But why, she asked, do they all carry such
horrible long knives? Indeed, the Western Americans do carry
the so-called Bowie knives, which they use in self-protection.
Alas, the unlucky ones who irritate them, when the Bowie knife
is drawn in anger or revenge. Now her husband entered the
room; as she had told me, he was suffering from fever. The poor
man looked worn out from illness and fatigue. We settled our-

---

[37] John William Tappe, from Hannover, filed for American citizenship in
1834. Daniel McCoy settled in the St. Charles district in 1797, when Missouri
was known as Upper Louisiana. He was a lieutenant of militia in 1804.

selves in the door of his cabin. As he told me of being the former owner of a guesthouse in Germany, his glances rested on the present poor surroundings. He said he would have a new frame house built in the fall. Then, as usual, the conversation turned to Duden, and Mrs. Teppe [Tappe] said reluctantly that this emigration fever must be a disease among the Germans that was caught also by her husband. With a sigh she asked me if I was going back to Germany again. I talked a while longer with the man, who seemed to be very brave and kind-hearted; then returned to Washington.

Wednesday, I was told, was the day the Germans were supposed to come to town to do their shopping and have a beer at Krüger's. Yesterday I talked to Count Benting [Bentinck],[38] Doctor [Frederick] Krug, and the famous shoemaker [Piers-teacher] who has rented the Duden farm for a few dollars and is now repairing shoes for the German farmers, with great success. The farm itself is in very bad condition. This man is a crank; he insists that nowhere has he had so much luck with his shoe repairing as on the Duden farm, and therefore he moved from the Von Bock farm. Doctor Krug explained the financial situation of the German farmers. Counts, barons, and all are penniless, he said. They work hard but are in considerable debt. Doctor Krug said that he, himself, was much better off in Germany, but he couldn't keep his mouth shut and therefore had to go to America.

---

[38] Count Bentinck, a year younger than Gustorf, came from Oldenburg, a free city about forty kilometers south of the North Sea. After he died, his widow returned with their daughter to Germany. Their son, a St. Louis apothecary, married the daughter of Henry Wellenkamp, who settled near Washington, Missouri, in 1839. Laura Wellenkamp Bentinck survived her husband and is believed to have remarried in Washington. Dr. Frederick Krug, farmer and community physician, emigrated with the Giessen Society. He was from Bavaria, and, like many other pioneers in the backwoods, he suffered a violent death; his carriage overturned near Augusta.

August 13. Four miles from here on the way to Union is a settlement of peasants from Osnabrück. About twenty families live on high ground. They settled here on Government land two or three years ago and are the lowest class of German immigrants. By constant diligence and hard work they now have large fields of wheat under cultivation, but they are lacking in domestic comforts and their homes are very dirty. I have never seen such dirt, even in the homes of the poorest squatters. On entering one of these huts, I noticed the large wooden shoes they brought with them from Germany, and I knew immediately where I was. The children, even the girls between the ages of eight and ten, were crawling naked in the dirt on the floor, and their beds were nothing but old rags. Torn shirts were hanging everywhere as well as long stockings. I saw chamber pots and dishes made out of tin. I addressed the oldest child in German and asked where her mother was, but she did not understand me. I then spoke to her in English with the same result. Finally she said: "Mother is gegangen water fetchen."

When the mother came she was so dirty that I found it impossible to drink the proffered water. I went to another house where a woman was running around in her underclothes, and if this was possible, she was dirtier than the first one. When I left this house I had to make my own path through a cornfield.

The long-anticipated but now anticlimactic inspection of the Duden colony, especially the farm occupied by Duden himself, was begun by Gustorf, accompanied by the elder Krüger brother and four other Germans, on his second Sunday in Washington. After crossing the river, their first objective was the hospitable home of the Von Bock family, where all Germans were known to be welcome.

The following morning the Von Bocks' guest set out alone to explore the abandoned Duden farm. He found it to be a desolate and deserted area, with few remaining signs of cultivation. Beyond the creek, clogged with rotting wood, was the spring that had been described in the Duden book. Behind a rotted fence was the shabby Duden cabin. On entering the ruined building, he encountered the German shoemaker with whom he had talked at the Krügers' store. Broken furniture and dishes, which once belonged to the controversial German writer, were scattered about the single room. Reflecting on the desolation about him and the fate of the many Germans who were influenced by Duden, Gustorf returned to the hospitable Von Bock home and thence to Washington.

The last visit in the Washington area was made on horseback to the farm of a former tutor of the Prince of Coburg. As his horse made its way along the path through heavy woods the visitor pondered over the manner in which time and circumstances can change people. "How can former professors, doctors, and lawyers who lived for fifty years among the highest and most cultured classes in Germany abandon that kind of life to become common farmers in western America?" he asked in his journal. But his genial host, Professor David W. Goebel, who had come from Sachsen-Coburg to rear his family on the western frontier of the New World, trusted in the beneficence of time and circumstances, for he told his visitor: "We old ones will pass away and rot, but our children, I hope, will have a chance to enjoy a new life in a new country."

Frederick Julius Gustorf's personal tragedy was that he, too, was forced by time and circumstances to abandon the only way of living that was compatible with his education and temperament in order to become a Western farmer, but he was not philosophically equipped to master the situation nor was he physically capable of doing the work of peasants. To the day of his death he struggled to retain the dignity and prestige that he believed were identified only with cultural, intellectual, and professional occupations. He did not live long enough to discover that his children were indeed able to get a good education in a wilderness with limited educational and other cultural facilities, that they did not grow up to be ruffians, and that they deeply appreciated the hardships and suffering their parents underwent on their behalf.

August 16. Last Sunday I crossed the Missouri, accompanied by the elder Krüger and four other Germans, our goal being a visit to the well-known farm of the Bock family. As a short cut, we left the road and traveled on a footpath through the thick of the bottom land, over fences, fallen trees, and through underbrush until we finally came to a dry lake. Our guide couldn't find the path across the so-called lake, and we almost got stuck in a swamp. With great difficulty and almost suffocating from the heat, we reached a small creek, which we bridged by placing trees across it.

Soon we saw the farm of Mr. [Wilhelm Johann] von Bock. We saw a small brick house in front of a mound, which was a welcome sight, because most houses in this part of the country are made of logs. I entered and was introduced to Mr. von Bock and his family. Madam Bock, a very cultured woman, surrounded by her five daughters, greeted me very cordially. I had heard that this was a very hospitable home where all Germans were welcome.[39] This was indeed a fact. The room was decorated with German engravings, a piano, and a small collection of books. It was filled with young Germans from the cultured classes, and the conversation was vivacious. They talked about a ball that had taken place in the house a few weeks ago, and also about the habits and customs of the Americans, which the Germans cannot get used to. We all refreshed ourselves with a strong coffee that was served in beautiful cups.

All this went on until evening, when a delicious dinner was served as well as a warm punch that put everyone in a mellow

---

[39] Concerning the Von Bock family, Gustave Koerner wrote, in *The German Element in the United States, 1818–1848* (A. E. Welde, Cincinnati), 299–300: "Enticed by the favorable reports of Duden and hoping to find the richest kind of land under a Neapolitan sky, a number of highly cultured families . . . settled near the forsaken estate of Duden, as early as 1832. We mention here only the family von Bock. The head of this family was a most charming and jovial, tho eccentric gentleman. . . ." And Herman Steine, a German immigrant who visited the Von Bocks on May 26, 1834, en route to the Duden farm, made this entry in his diary: "About noon we came to the farm of Mr. Bock who

mood. We then sang German songs. Darkness fell on this scene of jubilant German youth in an area that has been settled only a few years. When the guests were preparing to leave, my gracious host invited me to stay for the night, which offer I readily accepted because I was tired and did not want to return home in the dark.

The following morning, after a breakfast in the German tradition, I visited the farms of Messrs. [Edward] Simon, [Frederick] Münich,[40] and others; then Duden's "deserted hall." The latter, formerly occupied by Duden, himself, is now completely desolated and deserted. Here and there are signs of once cultivated fields. Farther on is a creek, clogged with rotting wood. Beyond that is a hollow tree and a spring which Duden described in great detail in his book. A few steps farther is a rotted fence, on the other side of which is the shabby Duden cabin. On entering the cabin, I encountered the poor shoemaker surrounded by his ragged children and all kinds of dirty utensils.[41] In front of a small broken window opposite the door sat the shoemaker. There was barely enough light to see the inside of the room. With no emotion whatsoever, he told me that one of his children had just died and that the Duden house was very unhealthy; therefore he plans to move a few hundred miles farther up the Missouri River. I could see that this German shoemaker was possessed of the roving spirit of the backwoodsman. I wished him good luck.

In the corner of the room stood the frame of a bookcase; all the glass was missing. Once belonging to Duden, this piece of

---

came from Braunsweig. In company with his son-in-law, Mr. Radsche, he has begun a whiskey distillery. Mr. Bock has a large farm and lives in a brick house. He intends to carry on the distillery business on a large scale. He is a wealthy man. We were cordially received and invited to stay for dinner, which we gladly did. The kindly features, the charming voice, and the cheerfulness of old Mr. Bock made a deep impression on me." *Missouri Historical Review*, XIV, Nos. 3–4 (April–July, 1920), 438.

40 Frederick Münch, also known as Muench, settled in 1834 on land adjoining the Duden farm. Although Gustorf mentions visiting "the nearby farms of

Messrs. Simon, Münich, and others" on his way from the Von Bock house to the abandoned Duden cabin, the casualness of the reference and the misspelling of the name here, as at the Dortmund auction, suggest that he was unaware of this man's cultural and intellectual influence upon the colony. Meeting and talking with Frederick Münch should have been a stimulating and enlightening experience that most certainly would have been recorded in the diary and probably would have changed the writer's impression of the motives of Gottfried Duden. That someone, especially Von Bock, did not mention his neighbor Münch to the visitor is difficult to understand. The elder Münch was born in the Duchy of Upper Hesse in 1799. After graduating from the University of Giessen, he became an ordained minister and succeeded his father as pastor of a church in Niedergemünden.

In the spring of 1834, Münch and his brother-in-law Paul Follenius each led a section of the Giessen Emigrant Society to the Duden colony. In *Der Deutsche Pioneer*, I, 243, Münch wrote: "After the close of the Napoleonic wars the population of Germany grew faster than the means of their support and employment could increase. The debts resulting from the wars, the standing army, the prodigality of the courts of the nobility, all these things imposed an unbearable burden on the people. The shamefully disappointed hopes for the Fatherland embittered *the best among us*. It was a time of general discontent and hopelessness. Just at this time Gottfried Duden directed attention to the new western states of the North American Union. This book is largely responsible for the fact that after 1830, thousands of our countrymen settled in Ohio, Missouri, Illinois, Indiana, Wisconsin, and Iowa." *Missouri Historical Review*, XVIII, No. 3 (April, 1924), 418.

The ultimate success of the German emigration to St. Louis and vicinity was recorded by Münch at the age of seventy-one years when he wrote, again in *Der Deutsche Pioneer*: "In the course of a generation Duden's dream has, after all, become reality, and also the ideals of the founders of the Giessen Emigration Society, to establish a new German environment in this Western part of the Union, has been fulfilled, though in a manner such as we had not anticipated or dreamed. By internal increase and by additions from the outside, Duden's settlement has grown, so that it now [1870] constitutes the geographic center of a German population extending over four or five counties." *Missouri Historical Review*, XVIII, No. 4 (July, 1924), 576.

[41] Steine, who had proceeded to the Duden place from the Von Bock residence, found the shoemaker Piersteacher and his family in residence. A former tenant had vacated the premises after one of his children had burned to death on the hearth during the family's absence. Steine made this interesting entry in his diary under date af May 26, 1834: "Many a German has been at that place during the last six years in order to see *where* and *how* that one lived, who with magic power has lured hordes of the sons of Germany from their dearly beloved but oppressed and mistreated fatherland, who with magic pen has clothed their wilderness with such a pleasing and attractive garment, and who has banished the fear of those who thought this was a country of Indians and wild beasts. How various are the feelings of those who followed his suggestions!" *Missouri Historical Review*, XIV, Nos. 3–4 (April–July, 1920), 439.

furniture was filled with broken plates and dishes. The most horrifying thing of all was Duden's fireplace—a big hole with a wooden chimney attached, and from the chimney came more daylight than through the window. I sat on an old bench, thinking about Duden and the fate of the many Germans who were influenced by him to emigrate to this country. So many of them were unfit for the life here in the wilderness, and they regret the day and the hour when their eyes and their fancies were captivated by Duden's fallacious accounts of America. The English have written similar books, but without the expansive influence upon the heart and mind, because the English are so cold and calculating and also they have more common sense. In his fancy the German saw mountains of gold where there was only lead; he dreamed of rich fields of grain and found only Indian corn; fat cows and healthy calves where there were only American swine.[42]

I returned to have lunch with the Von Bock family, including coffee and real German cream puffs. We spent a pleasant afternoon. There were a few more guests, the daughters of a trial lawyer named Weber. The youngest, I believe her name was Theresa, played the piano exquisitely and sang. I can hardly believe that women of such culture have come here to milk cows. The oldest and prettiest of the ladies told me that she was recently married to Mr. Behrens. We talked a lot about the English language and literature. At four o'clock in the afternoon I bid the Bock family a fond farewell and returned to Washington, this time taking the country road.

---

[42] Writing in the St. Louis *Westliche Post* on November 10, 1893, the distinguished Gert Goebel, son of Professor David W. Goebel, had this to say about Duden: "I who have lived more than sixty years in Missouri know only one man who knew Dr. Duden personally. This man is the old, venerable Doctor Elijah McLean who has lived a long time in Washington, Missouri, and who was on friendly terms with Duden, and often associated with him in the early days. This Dr. McLean often spoke to me about Dr. Duden and depicted him to me as a charming gentleman, well educated, and experienced in his profession. . . .

"Some time ago there was reprinted in the *Westliche Post* a letter which is probably very old. Among other things it contained an erroneous and unjust

137

August 18.   Yesterday I went on horseback to Newport, six or seven miles from here through dense woods. I came first to a horse mill; then on my right I saw a miserable, tumbled-down log cabin and an ugly red brick smithy. On the left were two or three log houses in better condition and a big brick building, the former court of Newport, now located in Union. It is presently occupied by the storekeeper. I dismounted, entered the store, and asked for a drink of water. Waiting for the water, I looked around at the farmers sitting on the counter. I heard the words *law* and *court* very often. They were discussing the case of the doctor who had killed a human being with a dagger and has been missing from his home in Newport ever since. I saw the dagger yesterday in Washington. Another doctor, half drunk, insisted that it belonged to him, and he was very pleased that someone had been killed with his dagger. He said he had left it in his office, where the murderer had obtained it. I drank the water from a tin cup, mounted my horse, and when the storekeeper bade me goodbye, I asked him how old the town was. To my great surprise, he said 15 years. "But your place doesn't seem to improve," I said to him. "True, sir," he answered; "they are making too many towns."

August 24.   It is almost unbelievable how time and circumstances can change people. How can former professors, doctors, and lawyers who lived for fifty years among the highest and most cultured classes in Germany abandon that kind of

---

estimate of Duden, and even accused him of having written untruths. Apparently the author of this letter must have been one of the many disappointed persons whose attention had been directed to Lake creek by the rose-colored account of Missouri by Duden, and which writer later discovered that it was after all no *dolce far niente* [do nothing], but that love for hard work, and perserverance, and a willingness to forego the comforts of life were the essentials of success here.

"The sad political conditions in Germany in the thirties of the past century were the cause which induced so many intellectual and patriotic men to emigrate to America. It so happened that Duden's book appeared just at this time. Naturally it enjoyed an enormous distribution and was read with wild en-life to become common farmers in western America? They think that they are philosophically equipped to master any situation, but they do not have the physical strength to do the work of peasants. They do not expect to get very far in their own lives, but are confident that their children and grandchildren will reap the benefits of their self-sacrifice. But I have my own opinions on this viewpoint, because how can children get a proper education in a wilderness without schools and other cultural facilities?

They will only grow up to be ruffians, and I seriously doubt that they will appreciate the hardship and suffering that their parents underwent on their behalf. Under the circumstances, how can anyone expect gratitude from their children? These were my thoughts when I was going to see Professor [David W.] Gebel [Goebel] yesterday.[43] He lives a few miles from Newport on Government land and came from Sachsen-Coburg. The path was overgrown with weeds and wound through heavy woods. It was no surprise to me and my companion, another German, that we got lost. After riding aimlessly for a while, we discovered a fence and decided to jump over it. We knew that we were trespassing on someone's property and were expecting to be reprimanded for our carelessness.

Luckily this property belonged to a German by the name of Braun, whose former home had been near Darmstadt and who knew Professor Gebel [Goebel] personally. Mr. Braun's farm, his shabby cabin, and the expression on his face were not encouraging. He was very thin, pale, and undernourished. His

---

thusiasm among the educated classes in Germany. Prominent men such as Paul Follenius and Friedrich Münch, who led the two divisions of the Giessen Emigration Society, were induced, with many other learned men, to follow in Duden's footsteps." *Missouri Historical Review*, XII, No. 1 (October, 1917), 4–5.

[43] Professor David W. Göbel was born in 1787, emigrated to Franklin County with Section II of the Giessen Society in 1834, anglicized the spelling of his name to Goebel, and became a dirt farmer in the wilderness. Dissatisfied with the rigorous and frustrating farmer's life, he moved to St. Louis, where he taught scientific subjects in public and private schools for several years. Then in 1849 he was appointed surveyor of Franklin County, which office he held for

thin legs were clad in a pair of rough linen trousers, and he also wore a very weather-beaten cotton jacket. His head was covered by a ragged straw hat, and from his mouth hung a German pipe. He was pleased to meet Germans and he invited us into his dark hole. There we found his wife with a baby at her breast. She complained that the Missouri itch had caused her feet to swell. After I was interrogated as to where I came from, what I had done in the past, and whether I was planning to settle, we continued our journey.

We rode another half mile to a small, nice new log cabin, which was the home of Professor Gebel [Goebel]. I addressed the woman of the house by asking for the Professor. Mrs. [Henrietta K.] Gebel, being deaf, referred me to her daughter, a charming eighteen-year-old girl who looked very attractive in her Saxonian costume. Mr. Gebel appeared, a most interesting figure with kind features and black eyes full of fire, spirit, and alertness. We talked about several subjects, all concerning the United States. When he heard that I had traveled considerably in this country and settled nowhere, he said: "Yes, yes, I can see that you will return to Europe." I suggested that southern France must offer a comfortable life, but he said his choice would be Austria, where the people enjoy a minimum of despotism.

The Professor, who was the tutor of the Prince of Coburg, was known in Germany as a strict republican. He has lived here in the woods only a few years and so far has cultivated very little land. His bare chest was quite tanned from the sun. With a

---

two years with his son Gert as deputy. When Gert was elected to the office of county surveyor in 1851, the elder Goebel resumed his teaching. Following the death of Mrs. Goebel in 1860, the Professor made several trips to his native land, the last one being in 1868. There he died in 1872. Gert Goebel, who evidently was not at home when Frederick Julius visited the farm, was born in Coburg in 1816. So far as his son was concerned, the father's hopes for the children of German immigrants, as expressed to his visitor, were fully realized, because Gert acquired more than an adequate education in the wilderness and became one of Missouri's most prominent citizens. His book, *Länger als ein Menschenleben in Missouri*, was published by C. Witter of St. Louis in 1877. His public service included two terms in the Missouri legislature. *History of Franklin County*, . . . (Goodspeed, Chicago, 1888), 572.

sigh, he said: "We old ones will pass away and rot, but our children, I hope, will have a chance to enjoy a new life in a new country." It was three o'clock and time to return home. I picked up a loaf of bread from the table in order to satisfy my hunger on our way back, but it was so bad I fed it to my horse. After a farewell and a handshake, we left the kindly professor and his charming daughter, arriving in Washington toward evening.

September 9. I remained in Washington until September 5th, then traveled back to St. Louis on the *Chariton.* The trip lasted almost three days because of the low water level of the Missouri River. Unfortunately, we ran aground on one of the frequent sand bars. After 24 hours of hard work the boat was refloated, and we continued our trip. Fifty-four passengers were in the cabin, and I had to sleep on the floor for three nights.

In St. Louis, the guest and boardinghouses were filled up. Since I didn't want to return to Staffelbach's place because of all the bugs at this time of the year, I honestly did not know what to do. Luckily I met my roommate from last winter, a goodhearted soul who once was a painter and now works as a clerk in a store. He had rented a room in a private house, and I was invited to stay with him. I have been sleeping on straw for several weeks, constantly [worrying about my unfortunate physical circumstances].

Thus ends the traveling journal of Frederick Julius Gustorf. The final entry, dated September 9, 1836, terminates with an uncompleted sentence at the bottom of page 128 of the original document. Page 129 was misplaced while the diary was still in the possession of the writer or possibly after it passed into the custody of his widow. A German friend of her husband's who read but did not translate the journal told Harriet about the missing page (or pages) in a letter dated December 14, 1881. The first letter to Harriet Benson, October 26, 1836, explains why the traveler decided to curtail his sojourn in St. Louis and return to the East Coast for medical advice and treatment as soon as possible.

A letter written to Harriet Benson, his Englishwoman, from Philadelphia on October 26, 1836, advised her of his decision to return to the East Coast for professional advice regarding his eyes. After apologizing for his negligence in not writing sooner and expressing the hope that she is well and in good spirits, the writer poured forth his loneliness and discomforts in the strange city.

Obviously having received encouraging words from Limestone Prairie, Frederick Julius wrote this interesting observation in December: "The uncorrupted heart cannot be content in these large cities, where folly and vanity reign uppermost, where nature, true nature, and all the noble train of feelings flowing from that very nature's source, must be, if not entirely slighted, yet greatly neglected. No, give me but one solitary nook in this wide world, and a being that understands how to sympathize with me in all my failings, feelings, and passions, and I am ready to give up all the world besides." And since "the being that understands" was his Englishwoman, it is not surprising that these words introduced a proposal of marriage. Thus, time and circumstances, earlier decried as negative influences, began to impose their subtle influences upon him.

Communication facilities being limited to stagecoaches in the winter months, the impatient suitor had to wait fifty days (like most lovers, he counted them) for Harriet's acceptance. When it came, he immediately prepared for his departure from Philadelphia as soon as the canals opened in the spring.

Since the death of his father, Frederick Julius had been contributing to the support of his mother, who was living in France. Now that he was to be married, he felt justified in discontinuing this contribution. With a sight draft on the United States Bank in the amount of 100 francs, payable to Mrs. Fredericka Gustorf through a Paris bank and dated February 9, 1837, he enclosed a note advising her that he was about to be married, that his annual income was only $300, and he no longer could send her any money. The news must have been received ungraciously, because Harriet recalled in 1881 that her husband's mother wrote him a letter just before their marriage which "gave him great pain."

Speculating upon the manner in which he would support his bride, Gustorf wrote his Englishwoman that they might be reduced to trade or other undignified means of support. Ironically, the man who had fled his homeland as a youth rather than yield to his father's wish that he become a tradesman, was to be forced by time and circumstances, despite his distaste for trade, to suffer the indignity of resorting to the "palpably material" occupation of frontier merchant as a means of supporting his family. Whether he would have tried to "sell calicoes or keep a fuddling grocery" is not recorded, but he and Harriet did return to Limestone Prairie from New Orleans a few days before his death with goods of an unknown nature with which he had planned to open a store in Peoria.

"Oh, Harriet, my dear," he wrote from Philadelphia as he was preparing to return to Peoria for the wedding, "you are right in saying: love is above wealth. I feel it now more than ever I did, since God has blessed me with that best of Fortunes: a person like yourself for a wife." In the same letter, Frederick Julius described the enigma of his situation in these lyrical terms: "I have wandered, I have roamed through a polished world, from my 19th year onward, and it seemed to me like a wilderness; at last I alight upon a real wilderness, and it seems to me like a world of splendor, for Fate has endowed that wilderness with a bright star, and that star shines but for me."

1

Philadelphia, October 26, 1836

My dearest friend,
    Wherever I tarried and whatever place I stopped at, my first
determination always was to communicate with you, but circumstances stept in and prevented me. When I left you, you will
recollect, my eye was still in a sad state and I suffered much on the
way to St. Louis, where arriving I stopped but a few days, and
immediately set out for Belleville as projected. There I consulted
Dr. Tiensch, but no hope. Four weeks passed in this way; I then
resolved to go to Washington on the Missouri, to hear what Dr.
Krug, another German physical rogue had to say. Here I was
detained about six weeks, found a great deal of relief, not from the
Doctor's prescriptions, but from the shady forests of Missouri. The
inflammation entirely subsided, but the sight was by no means
improved.
    From this place I wanted to write to you, but the nearest post-
office was ten miles off and I could not go myself. The cold weather
drawing near and being but poorly accommodated in a miserable log
cabin, after a long struggle with myself, not knowing what best to
do, I followed the blind impulse of my own feelings and went to
Philadelphia to hear what the rogues of doctors had to say here.
I consulted Doctor McLeland, one of the first Professors at the
Medical College. His opinion is that it might be operated, but as
long as I could see perfectly well with one eye, he advises me not to
do it, the affected eye being considerably improved by the all-
mending or all-destroying effect of Time. I have determined to put
a stop to it here, and do nothing at all for the present. But I think
I have talked enough of this tiresome subject, and this prating
about Self must be sickening to you, tho' I confess you had a great
deal of patience with me, tiresome fellow as I was then, when at
your house.
    No, my dearest friend or Harriet, if you will excuse the boldness,
do let us make up for being separated to such a great distance by
communing frequently with each other, and exchanging thoughts
on all and every thing that interests us. When I left Peoria, Mr.
Pennington told me of your being unwell. I hope it was but a slight

complaint and that you are perfectly well now and in good spirits. Wish to God I was the last! I am far from it; here I live in this large metropolis with not one single friend, surrounded by folly, vanity, luxury, and falsehood. Oh, that I could live upon an isolated island, with but one friend through life, I would very willingly resign the whole of this world, for it sickens me to the very heart.

How are you living, you and your kind brother, John? What are you doing, how thrives the farm, is your house improving, are you happy, are you content, all and everything interests me and therefore I beg that you will allow your pen free scope, for depend upon it, your words and feelings do not pass before a deaf ear and a frozen heart. As to myself, I feel that I am not a fit subject for these American cities or societies. Everything loathes me, and I feel happiest when within the four walls of my room which, bye the bye, is in a tavern where—you can imagine all the etceteras. The worst of it is that the winter already stands with his grim claws before one's door, and a person cannot always move where he chooses, or I would be off on the wings of a swallow. Times are very hard here; everything tremendously high and no money among the people. Only think, if I were to realize what little money I have out, I should lose about 800 dollars.

How is Mr. and Mrs. Pennington? Well, I hope. The kind-hearted lady, I fear she must suffer much in her log cabin by this time. But tell her to be of good cheer, things will be better with us all, depend upon it. There is a voice within tells me so.

With my kindest and best greetings to John, Miss Susan and the rest of the family, as also to Mr. and Mrs. Pennington and Captain Jones and family, I remain most affectionately

Your friend

F. J. Gustorf

a propos: Have you heard
    nothing of the Flowers?
    I did not since last April

2

Philadelphia, December 12th, 1836

My dear Harriet,

The delight I felt in receiving your letter of Novbr 19 you can certainly not imagine unless you place yourself in my situation in this lonesome state of a great noisy city, where all are hunting after some bubble or other, and the thinking man of reflective mind must needs remain wrapt up within himself for want of some sympathizing being that feels inclined to devote even one slight glance of reflection at the working within that stranger's bosom, yes, my dearest Harriet, every day I see and feel it more and more: the uncorrupted heart cannot be content in these large cities, where folly and vanity reign uppermost, where nature, true nature, and all the noble train of feelings flowing from that very nature's source, must be, if not entirely slighted, yet greatly neglected.

No, give me but one solitary nook in this wide world, and a being that understands how to sympathize with me in all my failings, feelings, affections, and passions, and I am ready to give up all the world besides! And now I will pronounce what often lay buried within my heart, when I enjoyed the bliss of being every day near you: Think you, my beloved, that, after sound reflection, knowing me as you must do, with all my failings and good qualities, if such I have, that you could be that being, and share my fortunes, good or bad, with me; think you so, then give me your hand and heart, and accept mine with all I possess in return for the gift, and become my wife.

But, my dearest Harriet, consult with your own self, let no person, no consideration whatever influence you; act from your own impulse, sound the inmost core of your heart, all the pros and contras, and see if you can live happily with me, or in other words, if you can truly love me throughout life, till death separates us to meet again in a better state of existence, I hope, than this terrestrial state. For, be our love ever so intense, ever so warm, and ever so firm against all the trials and changes of this life, yet attached as we are to this material state of existence, we are of course exposed to all the grievances and afflictions arising from the wants and requisitions, and daily demands upon us.

These should not pass through your mind unnoticed and should be thoroughly reflected upon. As I am not speaking to a green, unripe girl, but one, I am happy to know, whose mind is sufficiently matured to understand how to separate the true from the false, the real from the fictitious, the pure metal from the dross, there is consequently no need of particularizing, and my sentiments will be well understood. I am not what the world calls rich. I have been living these two years past on the small income of 300 dollars annually. Should you then accept my heart and hand and consent to become my wife, I should be the unhappiest man on earth if as such I should clasp you to my breast and not be thoroughly convinced that you are content, and the least of your wishes satisfied, for I should loathe to know my wife, my better self as I would call her, be no better than some of those American drudges to "sweat and grunt" through life. Harriet, I will go no farther. I have said I will not particularize. Think what love is when I say I love you truly, and you reciprocate that love by such as I expect from her who must be dearest to me upon earth, my all in all, the very essence of my life!!

As to the state of my eye, it does not trouble me too much now as a few months ago; I can also distinguish objects with it, if placed in a position where the light is damped or not too powerful. The spot on the pupil, tho' not removed, is not quite so thick or impenetrable as before, and several German physicians here are of the opinion that by applying more mercury upon it, so as to keep it in a continual state of inflammation, that spot might perhaps be absorbed in the course of time. I have tried it, but given it up again, perhaps to resume it. As long as the eye is free from inflammation I can read as well as ever, but not through a long spell of time. But, fearing to impair the eye, or rather wishing to strengthen it, I abstain from all reading except newspapers, which being everywhere dished up before my very nose, it is too tempting a mess to refuse for the very reason that a man may glance lightly over this light matter of American Incubation.

There is no possibility of traveling now—the canals being closed, and in the stage? Only think what horrors to be squeezed together with nine stout bodied fat Yankees, and transported thus to the "far west" perhaps half strangulated and wholly bespattered with saliva before one gets even beyond the Alleghenies. But I would bear all,

148

could I but travel with security to my eyes—I wont say limbs, which are often enough broken in these vehicles, as a matter of course. But what am I going to do this long dull winter, as you call it? I really do not know—it is enough to drive a man to madness. I advertised a few weeks ago that I would teach my own language, but tho' puffed up in the newspapers, but one or two fellows came to make some silly questions, and there it ended. I have given it up since.

You had another attack of the fever and ague; if you should have it again, which God forbid, I beseech you not to take any calomel, or better still, to take calomel in no case whatever. The people in this country, and partly in old England too, are too much addicted to the use of mercury, internally applied. You have no idea what sad effect it has upon the human system, and if you love me, abstain from it altogether. Our German physicians hardly ever make use of it. You may say you are strong. Permit me to say: no, I know better. You would be if you lived better, that's to say, if you took more nourishing food. I should never suffer you, as my dearest H, to live as you did when I was in Peoria. It is absolutely necessary for your constitution—and permit me to say that I know it—to live upon something better than a few crumbs of corn bread and a cup of tea, or some of your other lackadaisical messes. Dont be angry with me for speaking thus disrespectfully of your culinary things. Ascribe it rather to my ignorance as a Barbarian, a Goth or Vandal.

Now my best love to John, and tell him I am very happy to hear the harvest has turned out so remarkably well. Providence, or that all watching undefinable Power which pervades the Universe, harmonizing the whole, hardly ever fails in rewarding the industrious and those who are ever alive to the duties pending upon them. I am sure the corn west of your house must have turned first, for it was I that dropped the seed there; surely the boys or Emily must have recognized the particular spots in the abundance of stalks growing out of them, for verily I sometimes dropt more than five grains at a time; however it was done with no "mean propense." But, a propos the lattice [sic] to the left of the house, on the little patch which I dug, really or literally at the sweat of my brow, how did that turn out?—Certainly, mighty or powerfully, as Lord Dewsenbury— the fellow with lame arm you know, the mentor of soles [sic] —would have expressed it.

Writing this arouses my imagination, and with the help of

memory I find myself transplanted some thousand miles off into your chimney-finished kitchen where I find Susan busy preparing the rising, the unlucky woe-bringing rising; or I see her cutting off slices of bacon while poor Music and Keeper are wistfully looking up to snatch some thrown-off morsel of non-eatable. Oh, if Susan knew what I have done many times, how I trespassed against the ordnances issued by her! Shall I confide it? Well, many a time when the poor animals came stealing up to me, have I thrown them a piece of—meat, out of the ingenious and renowned waggen-cellar [sic]. What a difference between now and then, tho' I was then suffering, greatly suffering. I, who am and always was a passionate admirer of Nature, sweet nature, to be cooped up in one of those large American cities where, in a manner, everything deviates from nature; where, instead of fields, trees, plants, and the many other soul-stirring appendages, my eye lights on nothing but those cold and dreary-looking brick houses, and dirty streets, crowded with the throng of the money-making class. By Heavens, I would rather be in the company of old Dragon and the red-nosed cow, for tho' they do not speak, they look their sentiments, and I think I can understand them.

With my best respects to all the friends and acquaintances, I remain your

F. J. GUSTORF

N. B. Address as before, without squiring me.

3

Philadelphia, February 4, 1837

Mine own & dearest Harriet,

What a long tedious time intervening between my letter and
its answer! Only think, fifty days from the time I wrote, 1200 hours,
and if reduced into minutes, 72,000. By Heavens, I should think,
time and space enough to circumnavigate the whole known world—
in a balloon of course. But as our letters do not go in balloons, but
in snail-paced stage coaches, drawn by Horses, not infrequently
reminding one of that of poor Don Quixote's Rosinante, we must be
patient for the time being. But very fine indeed to preach patience
to others when we have got none ourselves, & I am one of those, so
that when I am anxiously waiting for something, I wish to possess
it already, when I am scheming something, that something shall be
accomplished already, when something is drawing near, be it storm
or sunshine, I long to be immerged into it already, without any care
or puzzling of the brain, for these last, I never could bear, which is
partly originating from the circumstance that during the more
active part of my life, and when moving in the sphere allotted to
me, every thing went smooth enough, & I never knew what real
crosses were. I hope and trust, my dearest Harriet, that with you as
my guardian angel there will be none neither. However, an entirely
new period of my life now opening, I cannot help passing sometimes
a restless hour or so, when involuntarily the thought strikes me:
Wilt thou and thy Harriet pass a cloudless life, wilt thou be able to
make her perfectly happy, situated as thou art with thy small
means? But then, I arouse myself again & bright hope darting its
beams from above, blots out the dark specks from the gloomy picture some evil spirit is drawing, and illumines the whole again into
one bright effulgence. But then again, Reason will maintain her
right & she scorns these flashes of the imagination, particularly when
darting forth in a country like this, which is the palpability of
materiality, when a man must be able to drive oxen, sell calicoes,
or keep a fuddling grocery. However, no more of this, & with King
Lear let me say: "Down adown ye!"

You ask me whether I "still believe that" you "should never be
content in any situation." I never believed nor expressed any such

151

idea, my dear, you must have misunderstood me. Perhaps I meant the situation I might be able to place you in, though I hardly know as yet myself what kind of a one that will be, whether the people will call you the storekeeper's wife, the farmer's wife, or worst than all, the grocer's wife. But no more of this: *C'est une chose dégoûtante pour moi d'être forcé de parler & de penser à la manière de la canaille.* Aaron Burr, whose memoirs I have lately been perusing, in one of his letters to his wife, says: "The language of the world sounds fulsome to tastes refined by the sweets of affection." We will digest a plan together, my dearest Harriet. All that I pray for now is that God may preserve your health and mine—which is very far from being what it once was—so that, when next I come, which shall be as soon as practicable, I may meet you in all the flush of health and spirits which, under existing circumstances, can be expected.

This business of administering, though I am sorry for the cause that should have brought it about, yet I say with you, as it must one day be done, better now and all at once, so that each may know what is his or her own, & so, I think, there will be no danger of seeing a future law-suit, or other disagreeable dissentions, which frequently turn up in such matters, arise out of this concatenation of circumstances. I suppose that the equal division you speak of also includes the landed property, this part of your letter not being explicit enough. But if the land is to be parceled out in equal shares, I dont understand how that part which is already improved & on which your noble mansion stands, is to be fared with. I am a poor head at expounding the law; you must therefore elucidate my dull pate on that matter. You wish the thing were over, upon my word, I should wish so too, were I in your place, for I hate quibbles of the law, & there is no law without them. However, you are a lawyer's daughter, you write like a lawyer too, & par consequence, everything must end to the satisfaction of all parties.

I am sorry to say the evil in my eye has not changed any either for the better or worse since I wrote you last. The cicatrix at the side of the pupil is the same, & the spot arising from it immutable and stationary. One Doctor advises to apply this, another that, & so I am sick of them all. The mercury, as mentioned in my last, I did not apply because in cold weather, as one cannot avoid exposing one's self to the air, it is rather dangerous, & so I concluded to wait *till the weather gets warmer. If I were in Germany, it might perhaps be cured with ease. The Doctors in this Land of the free are either quacks or empiricks at best. Another reason is that I fear to endanger the sound eye which, thank God, is so strong that I can now see almost as well as once with both. It is only in the evening that I suffer, not exactly pain, but a peculiar kind of pressure, or as if some insect were crawling over it. Writing or reading too much always increases this inconvenience. But on cloudy days, when the sun is overcast & I am in the open air so that the blood gets cooled, I feel and see tolerably well. But what shall or can I do? When I think of it, it makes me very unhappy.*

Then there is a rail road cutting from the Wabash to Peoria & across your monotonous prairie. Susan will be raving at me for being so saucy as to call the beauty of her prairie in question, particularly as she did once point out all its beauties to me in propria personae, & Jones, the Capitano, the hero of Waterloo, has been offered 18,000 dollars for his land. Fudge or fiddlesticks, as the Yankees say. I dont believe a word of it. I am certain it is much less; but as regards these rail roads, there is no end to the continual talking about them or planning them upon paper, like the many new towns, upon the sites of which there will perhaps be never houses enough for a very mouse to take shelter in. If all the canals and rail roads they say people are scheming in this land of cant & rodomontade should really be executed, there will be a canal & rail road to each farm house throughout the whole Union, and not a man will dare to walk or ride on horseback for fear of not being able to avoid the thousand locomotives that are crossing and recrossing his way. Well, when your rail road is done, Mrs. Pennington will be with you at one whiff. The devil! I wish there were one now, direct from my house to yours, how quick would I be in your arms, my dearest Harriet

Thine own
F. J. Gustorf

P. S. I will write again according to
your wishes, every three weeks
you say, but if letters should be
delayed, dont mind! a propos, is
there anything you want me to bring
on from here?

4

Philadelphia, February 8–12, 1837

Meine Herzens geliebte! There you see, I was thinking of you in my own native tongue, & that induced me to begin my address to you in German or Dutch, as the people in this country ignorantly call it. What if I had forgot that you do not know that lingo, & so had proceeded in that strain, to the no small edification of the beloved of my heart, which last is the actual translation of the above phrase, & which is thus rendered into English for fear you might be forced to call on the aid of the renowned—Dutch Henry, better still, be obliged to saddle old Fairy & gallop off to Peoria in order to hold a philological consultation with the Dutch baker's fat daughter herself! But fear naught, I will go on in your bonny good English, only trespassing occasionally against its orthography perhaps, for I am without Walker's or any other Dictionary. I see I am again getting into my nonsensical way of writing; but what the deuce can a man have to say who leads such a one-coloured life in this land of cakes and whiskey, who sees nothing checker'd except to take a stroll up and down Chestnut street where, as you know, all the beauty of the place conglomerates, & where the females nobly vie with each other who has the greatest abundance or longest feathers on her bonnet.

Hear and laugh! Yesterday, on a fine sunny day, I was thus promenading when two befeathered ladies were walking together, & conversing as usual very loud, and while thus engaged in the heat of conversation, the listening lady stopt short or stood still before some milinary [*sic*] store, while the talking one went on, & happened to come just near my side where, taking me for her companion, she went on talking with me, until all at once, turning to one side, she was almost frightened out of her senses on perceiving that her female companion was transformed into a whiskered manfish—as Goldsmith has got it in one of his fables—with great spectacles on his nose & rather of an outlandish appearance. She looked at me while I stared at her; she paused—then began to giggle, put on a bashfull look, thinking probably that I might have overheard all she said, whereas I did not pay the slightest attention, either to herself or to her talk, for my whole mind was with you at the moment, my dearest Harriet, she supposing however that I had

154

overheard the whole secret, if secret it be they were chatting about.

I have promised to write to you every three weeks, but I commence before that time. I will send you a kind of journal, or rather, I will write at different days and dates, this being the 8th day of February. It is evening. I wonder what you are doing now? I see you all in my mind's eye, sitting around the fireplace, & though a large fire, yet shivering to atoms. Aren't you, have I guessed right? By the Lord, I dont see how you can stand it in these Siberian winters in your nutshell of a house, & on the open prairie too!! I am sure it would freeze me to a very statue. No, my dearest H, give me a good stove & confound all your fireplaces!! How cold must it be now in the little chamber I slept in, where, I recollect, the wind came oozing through a thousand crevices, above, below, & everywhere.

February 9th, in the morning. I had a good mind to throw away what I had written last night into the fire. Why, I dont exactly know. Perhaps the melancholy fit that I am in this morning, & to which you know I am subject to occasionally, "will I, will I" was instigating me to such an act. But as the words stand, so let them stand. Such things constitute the mirror of a man's mind, & your Gustorf's should be known to you as it really is, without any varnishing or hiding. I have written but a few words & the spell of melancholy is off. There you see, my dearest Harriet, what benevolent effect the very thought of you has upon my moral being.

Yesterday I paid a visit to an old acquaintance of mine, a Mr. Furness, a Unitarian preacher & a complete gentleman whom I have known for some time, & in whose house, I believe I told you already, I was introduced to Miss Martineau from England, who, by the way, is now publishing a three volume work on America. Yesterday he introduced me to a Mrs. or Miss—I forget which, dont fear, even if she be a Miss—Morrison, I believe, who, as he stated before hand, was a German scholar. Let me tell you first, however, that scholars of any kind, & especially this kind, are my aversion. I would rather see at any time a plain honest fellow with sound good sense, than some of these literary gentry that prate about words while they think they are talking wisdom. Well, I was prepared to hear all that hackneyed trash and cant about Germany and German literature repeated over again, which I have heard so often, & which will do well enough for common-place creatures. But my heart and head are too absorbed just now with a weightier subject—you know what I mean—than to repeat or hear repeated all that stuff about Schiller, Goethe, etc etc. At first, Mrs. or Miss M said nothing on my supposing her to be a good German scholar, & that I was happy to find the ladies in Philada took a taste for our literature, & that I hoped they would go on cultivating it—tho' all this was said merely to say something.

But all at once, as common with some of the shes, she shifted her position, and began to appear modest or shy about the matter, & pretended to know but a smattering, or to have just dipped her fingers' ends into this pie of German compounds, or of Philosophy, perchance. But I saw that she was striving only to come round with greater eclat, & so I allowed her the pleasure. She told me then very mincingly: she had had two teachers, one she dismissed because he was a Pole—la pauvre Pologne!!—the other whose name was Klotz, she said, which in German means a knotty stick of wood, she did not like neither [sic], because his mind was too dull & he plagued her too much with grammar. Oh, poor dull-pated Klotz, I say, may God have pity on thy thick cranium, or the ladies will suffer thee to starve! The whole of this conversation had already begun to make me squeamish, so I shifted the dialogue from Schiller etc upon the drama, from that upon German actors, & from the last upon English actresses, & then finally upon Miss Ellen Tree, a first rate & quite classic English actress, whom, by the by, I saw perform, & perform, too, most splendidly, a few weeks ago.

After a panegyric for my part on the charming Miss Ellen Tree— English all over—I mean her and not my panegyric—my Rev. friend entered the room and put a stop to the whole talkation, for all walked off, & I of course too, not without, however, having been previously invited by Mrs. or Miss M to visit her. Well, shall I, or shall I not go? Perhaps she is—fallen in love with me? Ha, ha, ha, what shall I do? There is no other remedy but to tell her right out that my heart—well, Harriet, what shall I tell the poor larned sweat crater?—that my heart has been hit by a Cupid who lives not in the regions of Greece or Italy, but far, far in the backwoods, ay, ay, in the wild backwoods!

The 10th, 9 o'clock in the evening. What in the world can you be doing these long winter evenings? I really cannot imagine! You surely cannot be reading Jay's devotional exercises all the time! One wants something exhilarating too occasionally, particularly

156

when living so altogether without any excitement, as you must do, unless excitement it be when the tea-kettle upsets & wets the carpet; or the rising does not promise to mount as high as the Tower of Babel. What a summer-campaign is in the West, you know the opportunities I had made me tolerably well acquainted, but what regards such a campaign in winter, having spent the only one I was there in St. Louis, & not in the country [I do not know]. I am wholly obliged to make up for my lack of personal experience by drawing upon the fountains of my imagination. I can hear it now distinctly how the wind is howling most tremendously around your house; beating at the casements and rattling at every window pane, while the snow is coming down from above in dreary whiteness; in short, a complete storm.

But storm, snow, ice, hail & all that, what are they when one is snugly seated in one's room, close by a good stout hot stove, surrounded by hermetically closed walls where not one of the imps of the air can whizzle through! By the Lord, when I think of some of the cracked-up concerns of gouty houses in the far West, with their Herculean fireplaces, which, though they contain a whole forest of fuel, yet emit very little warmth, a shivering cold takes hold of my very vitals, and puts a stop to all farther ruminations. Quick, quick, get ye to bed my dear, for it is too dreary to keep up much longer! So good-night & pleasant dreams about eternal springs in gardens of Eden where Mr. Adam and his dear Rib neither knew of fireplaces, snow-storms, nor all the rest.

February 12th. It is no small task for one to write a kind of letter-journal, even to her or him who is dearest to the writer, for he has naught to say in this land of parched and pent-up feelings; nay, Abellard & Heloise [sic] themselves, if fate had thrown them together in this land of salt-fish & dried beef, would probably be as mute as a fish, & being mute, they most likely would have turned Quakers, & then the misfortune they complained of would probably never have happened to them. Do you know what business I may most likely begin, at least I am laying in a stock of goods already? Well, guess! But you will never hit it, so I had better tell you at once. Well—a spectacle store; for if I go on buying & exchanging spectacles, as I have done for some time past, I shall certainly have a good stock of it. A few days ago, I bought one of one man, but they did not suit me, so I bought another of another, & so on, so that by this time I have got some six or eight already. If you were here, I might ask your opinion about it, but you being not, *il faut être satisfait. Savez vous que je commence à m'ennuyer diablement dans cette ville?* Books that I wish to read, I cannot afford to buy; newspaper reading rooms, where I want to go to, they ask three dollars a quarter—too much for such trash of information. The Athenaeum which I like, & where I used to go occasionally this winter, having been introduced by Mr. Furness, my Unity-friend, I shall forbear from visiting any more, for the other day, on going out, a large bill, stuck up at the door, in which pay was demanded from strangers, whereas I was told strangers pay nothing, stared full into my face, & cautioned me not to show my tatter-demalion form again within its money-asking walls, for I cannot afford it neither, so tight is my pecuniary doublet screwed on.

The worst time I have is in the evening when I know not what to do. If the lights did not affect my eyes so much, I should go more frequently than I do to the theater. Last night I went to hear a Mr. Hunt lecture on Temperance. He is a little hunched-back fellow, Reverend too, of course, & did the subject complete justice. He is rather a witty chap, & knows how to make that subject, dry in itself, very moist, by his rich ebullition of sparks of wit & elucidating anecdotes. At the end of an exhortation to his audience about their abstaining from any kind of intoxicating beverages, he sent round papers for people to sign the non-drinking cause, when a lady handed me one of these to clap my name to it. I suppose I must have looked like a drunkard to her, as a matter of course in this land of groceries. Tonight, not knowing what to do or where to go, I mean to wend my steps toward the theater to see Hackett, the comic-actor. He is a Yankee, has already performed in England, & if I mistake not, was praised by John Bull, your compatriot.

In my next, my dearest Harriet, which shall be in a few days again, I will talk about this Hackett, like a dashing editor of one of those 40-column newspapers, & will talk & write so often that you may be induced to exclaim: for God's sake Mr. G or my dear G, if you can give me that endearing epithet, stop, stop, no more of this tra-la-la-la, or I shall ask you to write once a year. But a year! What a year?! No such thing!!!

God be with you, the wish of thy
Gustorf

Philadelphia, Febry 13th, 1837

My dearest Harriet, 60,000 pardons for the clumsy & awkward manner in which my last Letter was folded up! There was so much scrawled all over that I could hardly find blank [space] sufficient to write the superscription. Give me a sound thrashing for it, when once I am your Ladyship's devout & humble—what?—never mind, you will guess at it. How fond I begin to grow of that beautiful Yankeeism, to guess!

But now to what I have promised you in my last: Something on the histrionic art. Well then, I have been to see this actor. He is a man of no very extraordinary theatrical powers, and the reason of his pleasing in England is very evident. His forte consists in delineating the peculiarities, characteristics & oddities of Uncle Sam, or of the people of these United States, but rather more exclusively those which you see glaringly displayed in the West or in the interior of New England, among a certain class of people. But representations of such abortions of manners, customs & habits may please well enough in England, for the very novelty of the thing, & on a subject too, of which English travelers in this country have so often made mention in their itineraries. To see these things then taken from actual life, & held up before the "mirror of nature" cannot, of course, be otherwise than highly exhilarating to an English audience, for a short time at least; & this I take it to be the main reason of this actor's popularity in England. But I was struck with one observation I made that evening & which I think highly beneficial to the future improvement of manners in this country, & that is the patience & endurance with which the "groundlings" suffer themselves and their protuberances of faults to be publicly caricatured, when I know their sensitiveness on that head to be so great that even in private a man dared not to make mention of the least abominations in social intercourse. Among the pieces per-formed was *Jonathan in England* & *the Kentuckian*.

In the last piece there is a scene where a Mrs. Luminary is just seen alighting from England in one of the Hotels in the City of New York. She struts about in the parlour with tablets in hand to note down whatever of oddities she sees, saying that she came to collect information with regard to the manners of these "proud Republicans." (It seems to me that Fanny Kemble with her book

gets a hit here.) Nobody taking notice of her, her chamber maid
calls for a servant. A bowing, sneaking, cringing, yet familiar negro,
at last arriving, addresses her with Maam & some other "negar"
phraseology. She then enquires of him about a Mr. Freeman to
whom she has letters of introduction. The negro steps toward the
barroom to make enquiries about this Master Freeman, when the
folding doors being thrown open, you behold a mixture of all sorts
of people huddled together, some on the table, some on two or
three chairs at once, one with legs on the table, another dangling
them out at the window, some smoking, some chewing, some
spitting profusely & others reading newspapers with long "nives"
in their mouths.

The negro states that a lady wants to know about a Mr. Freeman.
Upon this they all, some 20 or 30 fellows, rush out to the parlour
upon the poor Mylady with burning segars in their mouths & puffing
most furiously into her very nostrils, so as almost to suffocate the poor
she; then stare at each other with vacant surprise, saying: "Freeman?
Freeman? Freeman? Why, I guess he is a merchant; I reckon he
lives yonder where you see that there store." In the midst of this
scene of prying into the lady & replying to her questions, bless me,
what think you should happen! why, the dinner bell rings, & all the
gentlemen rush out of doors, helter-skelter, some falling down in
the act, those behind over them, & a dreadful confusion ensues,
while the lady stands aghast & almost petrified with surprise at this
scene of hubub to secure good seats at the dinner-table. The curtain
drops & some of my neighbors in the pit regretted not to be able
to see them eat in effectiva [sic].

In another scene Mr. Nimrod Wildfire, the Kentuckian, intro-
duces himself to Mylady Luminary, for he sees no reason why he
must be introduced by others. He talks to her of alligators, horses,
buffaloes & the mighty Mississippi, & finally, as he is a stout, hardy
fellow, begins to think that she is smitten with his rubicund face, or
his prowess—for he is a mighty powerful boxer & fighter with the
long rifle. The poor Mylady is almost at her wits' end, when away
he runs in a hurry-flurry to fetch the parson to marry them right off.
There are some Englishmen too figuring in this play, one a great
rogue who wants to impose upon these honest Republicans by passing himself for some great English Lord, but through Wildfire &
Mrs. Luminary, with whom this mushroom lord had once a love

160

intrigue in England, & whom by no means he expects to meet here, his imposture is laid bare.

But if I go on with my critick [sic] I shall want half a dozen more sheets, besides I have forgotten some of the main intrigues already—so, good bye!

February 16. Well, Miss Benson, I have seen her, aye, I have seen her, vive la Bagatelle! Seen her? Seen what? What, Mr. Gustorf? Whom do you mean? Why, the lady, Mistress Morrison. But who is she, my dear Gustorf? Why, neither more nor less than a regular blue-stocking, a would-be-thought learned, in short, a petticoat philosopher. The silver bell at the door is rung, & a negro girl ushers me into the great parlour of the lady. Pictures at the wall, books on the table, before a splendid sopha [sic], attract my notice; among the first, one in particular, where a young beautiful female is pensively reclining upon her lovely arm, & apparently in a meditative mood, underneath the motto: "When to the session of sweet silent thoughts I summon up Remembrance of past times."

Remembrance of the past with me calls up so many thousand little things of various colours & shades that it always throws me into a peculiarly abstracted mood. But, bless my stars, she comes! I look round and the lady stands before me, all in a flutter, rattling away in a most ladylike manner about German philosophy, German poesy, German theology & German asceticks [sic]—meaning aestaetick—What German asceticks?! I could not help smiling within, & was very near bursting out right boldly by asking the good lady something about our a, b, c. But, for shame, Mr. Gustorf, you are too bad! But how can I help it when I hear our poor Germans called ascetick, who are such great sourcrout eaters and old hock drinkers!!! But to resume, she considers it nonsense to learn grammar; she argues thus: A person who is thinking & who wants ideas cannot bear such drudgery, which must be left to meaner minds. She talked, but truly I did not listen, for my thoughts were a woolgathering, & so, after having heard some more fiddle-faddle about larning, I took my leave—promising to give her a few lessons before my departure. Damn the dollars, a man cannot resist their bewitching influence, & so I must, will I will I, be bored with the sweet she by making the tacher [sic]!!

February 17. Oh, my dear Harriet, that you are not near me, or I near you just now, that we might have some conversation together. There are a thousand little & mighty things about ourselves I want to talk over with you, & to do it in an epistolary way is totally impossible & would weary out my patience, for months & weeks have I to wait before I can learn your assent or dissent, or your arguments in favor or not. Only think, 1680 Miles we are asunder; I have made it out the other day to a minute. It is night now. This was a gloomy day; the rain comes pouring down in torrents & forces me to stay in. Read I cannot, talk neither, for I have no one to talk to. Here I sit in the public room of a tavern, surrounded by a couple of tiresome fellows, the one an old bachelor, given to drinking, who is just now huddled up round the stove, sighing every minute: hey, ho, hey, for want of thoughts to occupy his mind; the other the tavern keeper himself, summing up his accounts of coffee, sugar, milk. Ah me, "a man knows what he is, but never what he may come to!" Sometimes, simply *pour me distraire*, I go down to a young German doctor, a clever fellow as regards education, but then shame to say, he lives or is obliged to live in the meanest & most vulgar of taverns. The poor leech, his money is gone to a cent, & as he does not know a word of English, his talents & acquirements will be of no great benefit to him neither. He now talks of going to work on the rail road & then find his way westward, to have a taste of the sweet corn bread & sweeter bacon, I suppose.

Now hear! This very man, so very learned & accomplished, shall I tell it you, oh horrid! This very man, out of despair, ennui, or God knows what, drinks a few glasses of punch too much, & in a fit of mania—throws himself out of the window. I come to him, find him in bed and his arm dislocated. Similar scenes have I seen in this country, & people are so foolish or priestridden as to ascribe them to wickedness alone, whereas the real cause lies too deeply hidden for such common-place minds to develop, & can be known only to wanderers like myself. But what are such things to you? Let us throw a black veil over them! My sheet is full, now I have written two letters since my last of the 6th. Will that do, or must I stop? Tell thine unchangeable & loving

Gustorf

I long for your letters & that very long ones. Pray take good ink & give my love to all the friends—if there are any—By the way I did not send the newspaper. Do you want one, tell me.

6

Philadelphia, March 3rd, 1837

My dearest H. Yours of February 7 I received while confined to my
bed by a very severe and painful Rheumatism in my right arm, the
same place where I had it last year in St. Louis, but there it was not
of such intensity of suffering as this spell. It began immediately
after I had written my last letter to you, and increased to such a
height that I was not in the least able to move my arm. I incautiously
applied 12 leeches to it, which kept my arm bleeding for 24 hours,
the pain is lessend, tho' my arm is stiff yet. Don't you be afraid, my
dearest; there is no danger of my dying of this. It will pass by, I
hope, with God's will. Don't you fret yourself about it and thus
injure your own health. If you love me, you will not. Dont you run
upstairs and cry, for if you do, my spirit which is always and ever
with you, will behold it, and thus you will increase my bodily pain
by adding that of the mind also. Now, once more I beseech you do
not fret yourself about it, for by the time you read this all may be
well again and, if not, there is no danger, it will only delay my departure for an indefinite time. I shall always remain true to you, and
love you with the same fervour, under whatever sufferings I may
labour or whatever your pecuniary circumstances; whether you have
only 164 dollars, as you tell me, or 164 cents, or no cents at all.

I can go on no further, for the exertion of writing, and writing in
bed too, pained my arm too much. As soon as the cold weather
abates I mean to try some warm baths, from which I expect real
benefits.

To the last gasp your true, faithful and unchangeable
Gustorf

Now once more don't take my transitory
state of suffering at heart, but be
merry and cheerful

March 7th

Dearest H. this letter could not go before,[1] having had nobody to
send it over to the post office. The pain in my arm is considerably
less, but the Rheumatism, I am sorry to say, has moved into my
right thigh, right in the joint, so that I can hardly walk. My arm is

[1] This letter, dated March 7, was enclosed with letter dated March 3.

so stiff and immovable in the shoulder bone that I can but with the greatest pain and exertion lay it on the table to add these few lines to what I have written before. Oh, that I am thus doomed to suffer!! Perhaps I ought not to have told you about all this, but, I hope, you have strength of mind sufficient to bear all this patiently without repining. Do pray, for God's sake and my sake, not take it to heart, but remain in the same mood as if you knew nothing about it—

          I kiss you in mind and remain till death your faithful
                                          Gustorf

7

Did you know—but you do—my dearest, my all upon this earth,
what exhilerating [sic] pleasure, what unspeakable joy, each letter,
nay, each sentiment of yours affords me, you would certainly have
written oftener this winter than you actually did. You have certainly
no reproach to make me on that score, for I have written you five
letters since last February, for which in return I received but one
today, dated March 4. It seems to me impossible that letters should
be so long acoming. Since my last which was March 12th I believe,
I wanted to write to you a few days after, but I dont know what
possessed me that I did not; I deferred it from day to day under the
only excusable plea, that I expected every morning to see an answer
to one of my five letters at least, and so 19 long days have elapsed,
during which time, my dearest and best, I communed with you only
in spirit and not by words, when at last my rascally landlord, to
crown the whole of this longing expectation, kept your letter 24
hours in his desk, having forgotten to deliver it before.

I could almost have torn the fellow, but that the perusal of it
allowed my passion time to cool down. But now, my dearest Harriet,
there is no more time, I fear, to receive another or others from you,
at least here, unless you have written again two or three days after
that I have now before me, for I am making preparations, earnest
preparations, to set out for the far West some time next week. Now
I beseech you, I conjure you, to do your utmost, your very best (for
a great deal depends upon the care you take of yourself) that I may
find you in good health, right hardy, strong, and in every respect
well, for—think not that I am exaggerating—it would break my
heart if I should, God forbid, find you otherwise. I shall not trust
your words alone in this particular, I must be convinced by eyesight
and, as a test, I shall make you walk up and down the hill between
your house and Pennington's, and without support of my arm.

Oh, Harriet, my dear, you are right in saying: love is above wealth.
I feel it now more than ever I did, since God has blessed me with
that best of Fortunes: a person like yourself for a wife. Oh, herein is
concentrated everything, by Heavens! to me it is. Oh, the thought
of soon, very soon, seeing you, embracing you, clasping you to my
heart forever, from which not even death shall separate you, if im-

mortality is no dream, which certainly it is not, has elicited tears from my seared eyes. I have wandered, I have roamed through a polished world, from my 19th year onward, and it appeared to me like a wilderness; at last I alight upon a real wilderness, and it seems to me like a world of splendour, for Fate has endowed that wilderness with a bright star, and that star shines but for me.

You did not seem to understand my quizzical allusions as to the Grocery; how could you otherwise, my dearest, for one moment have supposed me to be in earnest? Such matters are diametrically opposed to my taste, and they being so to yours is quite sufficient without any farther argumentation.

My health is tolerably well, so not quite as I could have wished it; when walking much I feel a kind of weakness or rather lassitude in my bones, which I attribute greatly to the effect of the climate in this hemisphere: For the transition from winter to summer—as to spring, there is none properly speaking—is too severe and trying to a European, or rather, Continental constitution, and mine is certainly far from being that of a Hercules. For instance, a few days ago it was almost cold, and last night we had a most tremendous thunderstorm, which followed upon a very warm, almost oppressive, day; it seemed to me at the time as if the whole artillery of Heaven had been summoned together to make a grand display, and thus usher in summer at once. Today it is cold again—But hurrah!—the canals are open!! Nobody but we two know how much meaning there is in that, and how the opening of a canal is connected with the beating of two yearning hearts! Last Sunday it was a most beautiful day, placid, serene, the whole atmosphere smiling—smiling like yourself when some kind benevolent feeling passes from your heart over your brow.

I strolled along the Schoolkyl [Schuylkill] and watched the fishermen as they were spreading their nets to catch the finny brood. Oh, that you were at my arm at the time! A whole bundle of fish you might have had for a nine-pence. There is no catching fish at the Kickapoo, is there? I have been thinking the other day: not having been on horseback for so long, what an awkward figure I shall cut when next I may bestride Buck, Dragon or the Devil. I hope Fairy will be more "gently" (your own word to her) under me, for she will certainly soon find out that I'm no longer a stranger, but one connected by indissoluble bonds of heart and mind to her kind mistress, my sweet Harriet. Fairy is an animal of much sense or spirit and she will soon find that out. I am always ashamed to appear near you, my dear, I mean on horseback, for you can do it so very much *en cavaliero* and with so much becoming grace; while I must have looked to the good folks in Peoria like Sancho Panza upon his ass.

I am glad the auction is over. What a fuss there must have been in the house with all the colonels, captains and Squires; the Dewys, the Dewsenburys and the Henrys. Going, going, gone! the book is knocked down to Mr. Dewy, Esquire. What, that philosophical work to Mr. Dewy, the mender of old soles?! Aye, aye, he is going to turn parson and mend souls in future. The fellow makes me laugh when I think of him. By the way, last week I had a letter from Mrs. Flower, the first letter since those I showed you, you recollect, before I had had the pleasure of even having seen you. I now may tell it you: When I put up at Peoria, I asked the landlady: "Do you know Miss Harriet Benson?" "Know her," she replied, "oh yes, she is an excellent girl, every body likes her." Since that time I have always liked that woman, and I have several times even called upon her in Peoria, since. But, Mrs. Flower's letter! Well, it was a very long one, but seems to me to have been written to settle the enquiry whether 1000 German hands could be had here to work on their rail road. She talks a great deal about her children and a long tirade about the happy pair whose wedding festivities lasted I don't know how many days, which set all Albion in an uproar. I consider that nonsense to say the least of it. We, my dearest Harriet, will have no such fuss at our nuptials, but all in quiet and among ourselves. But am I not already wedded to you by bonds of mutual heartfelt sympathy and everlasting love and affection, more than church ever can do?

Good bye, till to the happy moment of meeting. Thine to eternity
Gustorf

As I may probably stay a few days in St. Louis to see some of my German friends there, I request you to let me find a letter from you at the post office, immediately after my arrival there, and you shall have another from me too, but under the only condition that I do really find one from you. Now mind, my dear, or I shall punish you with—50 kisses.

8

Off Portsmouth, April 22, 1837

The last letter I wrote you, my dearest Harriet, was from Philadelphia April 7;[2] when I left on Monday morning April 16th, arriving at Pittsburgh at the dusk of even, at which place finding a
steamboat immediately ready to start, I did not tarry one moment,
but went right on Board her for Louisville, Ky. Now thanks unto
God, I am some 500 or 600 miles nearer to you and hope soon to be
with you, my dearest, altogether, tho' in mind and soul, I have been
with you ever since I left you. Oh Hope sweet Hope, & sweeter
prospects of Futurity, which, with God's blessing, I flatter myself
of being realized, & realized to the goblet's brim. Wont it be so, my
dearest Harriet, my only consolation after the manifold trials and
vexations I have gone through in the labyrinthine paths of this
trying world! We have had a pleasant or rather I ought to say a safe
journey thus far, with the exception of some difficulty in crossing
the Susquehanna on account of a bridge having been torn away by
a freshet; however we weathered it out, as you British sailors say.

My fellow travelers too are the politest, kindest & pleasantest set
of Yankees I have yet met with on my travels, or in your western
world with her backwoodsmen & backwoodswomen (are you one
too by this time, my dear?) when such company is a scarce article—
almost as rare as to find another Harriet—we know much more how
to appreciate such a lucky chance. We—these folks and myself—
agreed to travel together as far as St. Louis, & by so doing we save
some 8 or 10 dollars, which you know is something to Our (by our
I mean yours as well as mine, which may seem a paradox to you tho'
not at all to me) purse. I am sorry, however, on one account (is
there any cause for being so?) for my immediate departure from
Pittsburgh & it being too late, prevented my executing Pennington's
beer or ale commission, & the poor John Bull will needs be forced
to drink water from the pure fountain instead of the brown jack you
English folks love so much.

How can he or anyone expect that I should put off or delay that
precious time which is to bring me nearer & nearer unto you, for
3 or 4 days—for a mere beer barrel!! No, far better to drink his wife's

2 This letter either failed to reach its destination or, for some reason, became
separated from the other and lost.

168

health from your current spring & put off the beer notion to some other opportunity, and be careful in future not to give his orders to a fellow who is love-struck as I am. Beer & love, how clashing, how unharmonious!! Were it Lamian wine or some other term connected with sweet & endearing associations, the thing might perhaps do, but beer & love, beer & love again, it grates upon my very teeth!!!

Today being Sunday, what think you my future wify, has happened to your future "Old Man"? I am sure, nay I would wager my very life's blood, did I not know it was dear unto you, that you will never for a moment divine it. Well, what think you? Shall I leave your curiosity unsatisfied, upon the stretch till we meet, or tell you right out? But nonsense, to ask of a lady, tho' a lady dear, to suppress her curiosity! So, to it then: The Bostonians, my fellow travelers, as clever and well educated a set of fellows as ever you or I met with in this land of Democracy—I am a true Republican, for all my railing at the stuff occasionally, & depend upon it, you will never get me to pray for a King, but for a Jackson neither—came to me this morning being Sunday, & requested me to give them a— what, what, what, out with it Gustorf, you rascally chap, your impatience will make you say—of course, against your heart's desire —well, a Sermon. Now, laugh or smile, my orthodox Harriet, at this idea of my turning turn-coat & put on the phiz of a devout hysterical Methodist parson.

I laughed myself at the idea, but within my sleeve, like Mephistopheles while haranguing the theological students in "Faustus." But, you my dear, knowing nothing about this latter, I will talk no more about myself, the parson & the Yankees. You will have one for your husband, but never for your Bishop, I "guess & reckon," wont you? But one story more, a better one however, & more to your gusto. I am in a stateroom with one of the above Bostonians. He sleeps in the upper, I in the lower berth. So last night, after having played a round of whist, I retire to bed, it was about 11, and am surprised to find the light still burning & my chum wide awake with something in the form of a duodecimo in his hand.

Upon my asking him what he was reading at so late an hour, his reply was: "Something that's very pleasant reading," and he showed me a miniature picture of his Dulcinea in Boston. I look at it, & to my surprise find some slight resemblance with my dear Harriet's countenance: her mouth, her lips, tho' not her eye—the eye, the eye which is all in all, for it speaketh the image of the soul & reflects its inner qualities, those qualities that are ethereal & not material, those that are lasting & not fading & tarnishing with Time, the spoiler of the mighty works of the creation.

At St. Louis I hope to find letters from you, for you owe me four letters yet and I wont credit you much longer, if you dont pay me half the debt at least. The answer to this, I shall receive from your own lips; lips upon lips, mute, yet saying much, for both inhale at the same time what the soul feels—for no words can give it. Is it not so, Harriet? I don't expect to stay long in St. Louis & then farther on to Peoria! I see you already standing at the kitchen door, awaiting my arrival. I hope you wont be away from home, at Mrs. Jones or Mrs. Somebodyelse. Fairy, bear thy Mistress well and speedily when she comes to meet her true & faithful

Gustorf

P. S.   The continual shaking of the steamboat prevented me from writing better or more legibly. My compliments to Susan & let her have the dumplings ready & by all means well done! No offense I hope.

Harriet Benson and Frederick Julius Gustorf were married at the Benson home on Limestone Prairie, September 13, 1837. He had left Philadelphia on the morning of April 16, arriving at dusk in Pittsburgh. There he found a steamboat ready to depart for Louisville, and he went on board immediately. A letter written off Portsmouth, Ohio, by the impatient passenger on April 22 was mailed the next day at Cincinnati. Of the nature of his business in St. Louis, other than to see a few German friends, as he told Harriet, there is no record. Nor is there any clue to what further thoughts he entertained on the manner in which time and circumstances can change people as he approached the scene of his own transformation.

Although God had blessed him with "that best of Fortunes," a person like Harriet for a wife, and the couple had agreed that "love is above wealth," the loss of his Frankfurt savings deposited in three Philadelphia banks and the annual income derived therefrom was a catastrophe. This happened in 1838, their first year of marriage. "You can imagine his anxiety for the future of his family," Harriet explained in 1881. "I had land, a part of which he tried to cultivate, but this was laborious and unprofitable without means to carry it on. So in 1844, when we had three children . . . he concluded it would be best to sell the land and the town lot in Peoria I had inherited, and return to Germany. I had received a very liberal education, and we thought that together we might establish a school.

"We went as far as New Orleans, remained the winter where my husband had classes in German and French; but decided, I do not know why, not to go to Germany but to return to Peoria and open a store, having invested his money in goods. We arrived in Peoria on June 7, 1845, went out to my Brother's house eight miles in the country, and there he died of colic caused by drinking too freely of cold water when very warm. He lived but a few hours after first taken, although the physician had given me no hint that it might terminate fatally."[3]

As for the store in Peoria, Harriet did not indicate whether her

[3] Frederick Julius Gustorf's terminal illness was cholera, not colic, as Harriet advised his nephew in Cöln. Presumably he caught the dread disease from rats that infested the steamboats on which they traveled from New Orleans to Peoria. Possibly the widow's memory slipped a little over the years, although for a woman of her integrity and alert mentality such a lapse seems unlikely. Aware of the frustrations, disappointments, and indignities that her husband had suffered during the years of his maturity, perhaps she sought to spare his memory what she may have considered to be the ultimate indignity.

husband had planned to "sell calicoes or keep a fuddling grocery."

Frederick Julius Gustorf is buried in Limestone Township, seven miles from Peoria, in the cemetery of Christ Church, which was consecrated in December, 1845, the year of his death, by the Right Reverend Philander Chase, Bishop of Illinois. The Bishop's certificate, written on the first page of the church record, reads as follows:

I hereby certify that on the 10th day of December, AD 1845, this Building called Christ Church, Lower Kickapoo was duly consecrated to the worship and Service of Almighty God according to the Liturgy and canons of the Protestant Epis. Church in the United States of America by me

PHILANDER CHASE
Bishop of Illinois

The Reverend John Benson, Harriet's brother, became the first permanent rector after being ordained by the Bishop. He served in this capacity from Easter Sunday, 1852, until November, 1857.

The little church was built of native limestone and walnut at a cost of one thousand dollars, of which one hundred dollars was contributed by Her Gracious Majesty, the Dowager Queen Adelaide, widow of William IV of England (d. 1837), and a like amount was given by Lady Alicia Lambart, who also helped to raise an additional three hundred and seventy dollars among her friends, including one hundred dollars from Lord Kenyon.

A bell tower was added to the structure in 1880; ten years later the plaster ceiling was removed and the rough beams were boxed. In 1937 the old building was restored, and for many years thereafter annual services were held there in memory of its founders. More recently, a group of interested families prevailed upon the Bishop of the Episcopal Diocese of Quincy to reactivate the parish as a diocesan mission with a member of the Cathedral staff as priest.

The eldest of Harriet's three children, Frederick, was six years of age when their father died. Unfortunately, Frederick Julius was deprived of the pleasure and satisfaction of sharing with their mother the responsibility of the children's education and the inevitable discovery that firm parental supervision, spiritual guidance, and loving care are just as important in rearing a family, whether in the wilderness or in Boston, London, or Frankfurt, as formal schools and other cultural facilities. On her seventy-second birthday Harriet, who did not remarry, expressed her views on the care of children to her son Frederick and his wife Sarah Collins, as follows:

"God bless you my Beloved son. You and Sallie have given me a good and happy House and from my inmost heart I thank you both. May God bless you in the love and devotion of your Children. You have also spared of your means when you could ill afford it, to give regularly to me, and I know God will bless you for it. He has blessed me and He will you. In this age it requires firmness and the Help of God's Grace to bring up children properly. May you, my dear Son, seek that Grace and be guided by it. Do not let your judgment give way when you are coaxed to allow what your better judgment disapproves, and depend upon it, your children will bless you in the end."

It is acknowledged that the character and personality of Frederick Julius Gustorf probably are of greater interest to his descendants than they will be to the historians. His *Traveling Journal*, however, is historically significant because of his extraordinary power of perception and the original manner in which he responded to everything that stimulated his curiosity. The romantic reader will be fascinated not only by the traveler's preoccupation with the natural beauty of the American frontier, especially the Allegheny Mountains and the Ohio River Valley, but also by the fact that his literary effort remained unread and unpublished for one and a quarter centuries. The historian will recognize many frontier scenes, customs, and conditions that were observed and publicly recorded by Charles Dickens, Francis Lieber, the much-maligned Gottfried Duden, Miss Martineau, Alexis de Tocqueville, Isadore Löwenstein, and other contemporary European travelers in North America.

But many things to which his imagination reacted had their own historical uniqueness, like the horse-powered *bratwurst* machine and the Clopicki boardinghouse in St. Louis, the "infernal regions" of the D'Orville museum in Cincinnati and the auction of lots in the nonexistent town of Dortmund on the Missouri River. For those who are interested in the agricultural development of the Illinois-Missouri frontier, Gustorf's voluntary apprenticeship in prairie farming at Albion and his interviews with farmers at Belleville and Washington provide an authentic appraisal of the exhausting work required of those who sought to live by cultivating the soil and the extreme hardships they encountered in backwoods living.

"A farmer's life," he observed, "is neither romantic nor idyllic; just hard work with small rewards." And on the farms as well as in the towns he noted with grave concern how many of the culturally starved Europeans were "taking refuge in the whiskey bottle and trying to give an impression of gayety," but unhappiness, homesickness, and discouragement were written on their faces.

Index

175

176

Peck's *Gazetteer*, 63
Peking [*sic*], Illinois, 94
Pennington, Mr. and Mrs., 145, 146, 153, 168
Pensoneau, W., 112
Peoria, Illinois, 45, 73, 89, 91, 94–96, 103, 105, 107, 144, 153, 171, 172
Peoria Light House, 97
Persico, Luigi, 11, 11*n*1
Petersburg, Pennsylvania, 13
Philadelphia, Pennsylvania, 8, 143, 171
Pickering, 48
Piersteacher, 135, 136
Pittsburgh, Pennsylvania, 10, 11, 14, 15, 17, 168
Portage des Sioux, Illinois, 92
Portsmouth, Ohio, 23, 171
Prairie House, St. Louis, 84
Prescott, Samuel J., 6
Press and Fatherland Society, 118

Q   Quakers, 157
     Quincy, Illinois, Diocese of, 172

R   Radsche, 135
     Rafauf, 107
     Rapp, George, 42
     Reus, Adolph, M.D., 109
     Rheinbayern, Germany, 3
     Rice (Reiss?), 27
     Ridge Prairie, Illinois, 66
     Ridgeway's, 61
     Rockport, Indiana, 40
     Römerhill, Frankfurt/Main, 7
     Rosengarten, G. D., 5, 8

S   Sachsen-Coburg, Germany, 132, 139
     Sack [*sic*] Indian, 82
     St. Charles, Missouri, 86
     St. Charles County, Missouri, 86
     St. Clair County, Illinois, 109
     St. Gallen, Switzerland, 69
     St. John's Creek, Missouri, 128
     St. Louis, Missouri, 19, 63, 67, 89, 91, 96, 103, 106, 107, 141,
          157, 167, 168
     St. Louis Republican, 78
     Sallie. *See* Sarah Collins Gustorf
     Sawyer, John York, 64
     Schnelz, Martin, 31
     Schnurgasse, Frankfurt, 7
     School and Church Commission, Frankfurt, 7
     Schott, Anton, Ph. D., 109
     Scioto River, Ohio, 23
     Seume, Johann Gottfried, 103
     Shiloh, Illinois, 117
     Shippingport, Kentucky, 39
     Simon, Edward, 136
     Snyder, Adam W., 117
     South Point, Missouri, 122
     Spoon River, Illinois, 101
     Spring, Dr. Archibald, 50, 51, 53, 56
     Steffelbach's boardinghouse, 91, 113, 141